POLITI

D0575135

JUL 22 1991

HOTSHOTS

Baseball

GREATS OF THE GAME
WHEN THEY WERE KIDS

SUSAN SLOATE

A *Sports Illustrated For Kids* Book

First Edition

Library of Congress Cataloging-in-Publication Data

Sloate, Susan.
    Hotshots : baseball greats of the game when they were kids / Susan Sloate.— 1st ed.
        p.   cm.
    "A Sports illustrated for kids book."
    Summary: Describes the childhoods of Babe Ruth, Mickey Mantle, Nolan Ryan, and others whose persistence, practice, and love of the sport turned them into baseball hotshots.
        ISBN 0-316-79853-3
        1. Baseball players—United States—Biography—Juvenile literature.   [1. Baseball players.]   I. Title.
    GV865.A1S518   1991
    796.357'092'2—dc20   90-46520
    [B[920]

SPORTS ILLUSTRATED FOR KIDS is a trademark of
THE TIME INC. MAGAZINE COMPANY

Sports Illustrated For Kids is a joint imprint of Little, Brown and Company and Warner Juvenile Books. This title is published in arrangement with Cloverdale Press Inc.

10 9 8 7 6 5 4 3 2 1

RRD OH

For further information regarding this title, write to Little, Brown and Company, 34 Beacon Street, Boston, MA 02108

Published simultaneously in Canada by Little Brown & Company (Canada)

Printed in the United States of America

Interior design by Harold Nolan

CONTENTS

People have been playing baseball in America since the early 1800s.

INTRODUCTION

Baseball is America's favorite game. We watch it, play it, we even argue about it. And some of our biggest heroes are the game's superstars—the "hotshots." Who is a baseball "hotshot"? Who are the players who have left their mark on the game? Are there any qualities they have in common?

Superstar pitcher Tom Seaver once said, "You try for success by using four elements: hard work, dedication, concentration and God-given natural talents." Those qualities (and sometimes a little good luck!) separate the great players from the hundreds of others who come and go without making a significant contribution to the game.

Of course, no player becomes a hotshot just by stepping into a major league ballpark. Sometimes you can spot the potential hotshot in his childhood. If you look closely at a star player's early life, you may see signs that he's on his way to superstardom.

The boys who grow up to be baseball hotshots often model themselves after an adult they admire, perhaps a father or an older brother who teaches them how to play. They tend to be more persistent than other boys. They work hard to sharpen their baseball skills. And oh, how they love the game!

Not all the hotshots have led heroic lives off the field. Some have made mistakes or done things they later were sorry for. There are players who have had problems with drinking, drugs and gambling. Still, when it came time to play ball, the hotshots always gave their very best.

Here, then, are the early stories of some of baseball's greatest heroes—where they came from, how they grew up and what started them on their amazing careers.

Joe Tinker (left), Johnny Evers (center) and Frank Chance (right) were the Chicago Cubs' famous double play trio.

Christy Mathewson of the New York Giants was inducted into baseball's Hall of Fame in 1936.

Cy Young is the only pitcher in history to win 200 or more games in both leagues.

THE EARLY STARS

1

Baseball was a popular American game long before the Civil War. At that time, though, there were only a few teams, most of them in the Northeast. During the war, Union soldiers taught Confederate prisoners how to play. When the war ended, baseball teams sprang up all over the country. Soon teams were traveling long distances to play one another. Year after year, baseball drew more and more fans to the parks.

Shortly after the turn of the century there were two separate major leagues—the National League and the American League. During the regular season, the clubs of each league played only other teams in their league. At the end of the season, the pennant-winning team in each league faced each other in the World Series. In the first World Series, played in 1903, the American League champion Boston Red Sox defeated the National League champion Pittsburgh Pirates.

By the early 1900s, baseball was America's favorite sport. Talented ballplayers became famous. There were hard-throwing pitchers like Walter Johnson, Christy Mathewson and Cy Young. There were brilliant fielders like Honus Wagner, and the exciting double-play combination of Joe Tinker to Johnny Evers to Frank Chance.

There were also great hitters, and none were as great as Babe Ruth, Lou Gehrig and Ty Cobb. They were in a class by themselves. These three spectacular stars were the true hotshots of baseball's early years.

Babe Ruth was known as "The Sultan of Swat."

THE KID FROM THE DOCKS

He wasn't really a bad kid. There just wasn't anyone around to teach him the difference between right and wrong. So seven-year-old George Herman Ruth, Jr. had been sent to St. Mary's Industrial School in Baltimore, Maryland. Even at that early age, he was listed as "incorrigible," a boy who wouldn't follow rules or respond to discipline.

The year was 1902, and St. Mary's was filled with such boys. Some of them, like young George, were problem children. Some were orphans. Some were runaways. Some were just unwanted. The priests who ran the school treated them all the same. The priests gave the boys shelter, fed them and taught them each a skill that could be used to earn a living in the outside world.

One of the teachers was Brother Matthias. In addition to his classroom work, he was in charge of organizing sports at St. Mary's. One day shortly after George arrived at the school, he watched as Brother Matthias gathered a group of older boys around him, gave the boys some instructions and sent them out onto the baseball field.

The priest stood at the other end of the field. He tossed a baseball in the air and then swung—*hard*—at it. The ball flew off the bat high into the air, and soared over the centerfield fence 350 feet away. It would have been an amazing hit for anyone, but it was especially so because the baseballs donated to St. Mary's were old, lumpy and lifeless. The boys had a hard time hitting them 50 feet, let alone 350!

As George watched, he felt something come alive inside him. He wanted to be able to hit a baseball as far as Brother Matthias. From that moment on, he had a goal.

Of course, Brother Matthias did not introduce George to sports. That introduction had come on the Baltimore waterfront, where George was born on February 6, 1895. He was the third child in a very poor family. His parents, Kate and George, Sr., were too busy running a saloon near the waterfront to pay much attention to him. His older brother, John, died when George was a toddler, and his older sister, Mayme, couldn't manage him.

Young George spent his time in his parents' saloon or on the streets. He played with older boys, who used rough language and often committed small robberies. They also introduced him to sports, though not in the usual way.

George learned to swim when the older boys heaved him into the icy Patapsco River without warning. He learned to catch while watching them stand in a circle, tossing around a burlap bag filled with stones and sand that served as a crude ball. Sometimes when they threw the bag, George would dart in front of them and catch the bag himself. The older boys often beat George when he grabbed the bag, but the little game also made him quick and competitive.

By the time George turned seven, Mayme knew she could no longer handle him. He wandered in and out of the saloon whenever he liked, swore, chewed tobacco, stole small objects and spent most of his time with the tough, older boys. Mayme couldn't continue to act as substitute mother for George, and he was rapidly getting out of control.

In June of 1902, George was sent to St. Mary's. He stayed there only a month before his parents decided they missed him and wanted him back. However, Kate and George, Sr. didn't have the time or the patience to look after their son properly, and four months later, he returned to St. Mary's. A month after that, his parents moved to a better neighborhood and once more they brought him back to live with them.

But the arrangement did not succeed as well as they had hoped. Two years later, in 1904, it was back to St. Mary's for nine-year-old George. He went home again in 1908, then returned to St. Mary's after his mother's death. He went home in 1911, and returned to St. Mary's in 1912.

The other boys in St. Mary's thought of the school as their home. They made friends with each other, and learned to respect their teachers. But George spent so much of his time shuttling back and forth between St. Mary's and his family that he couldn't develop the friendships that might have made him happy.

What he did develop, thanks to Brother Matthias, was a kind of discipline. Each boy in St. Mary's was taught a trade so he could earn a living in the outside world. George learned to be a tailor. He spent many days, under Brother Matthias's direction, preparing and cutting fabrics on long, scarred wooden tables. He knew exactly what he would do when he grew up: He would leave St. Mary's at the age of 21 and go to work as a tailor somewhere in Baltimore.

George also developed great athletic skills. Brother Matthias had observed George's natural talent for throwing, catching and hitting those sorry, lumpy baseballs, and the priest spent extra time patiently teaching George everything he knew about the game. George learned quickly and worked hard and soon began to play baseball with the older boys. George was a much better player than the kids his own age.

The older boys learned that George was as quick and as agile as they were, and that his baseball instincts were excellent. Though he was younger than they were, he was rapidly filling out and growing taller. Thanks to long hours of practice, he had become a good catcher, the position he played most often. But one day, when George was 15, St. Mary's ran out of pitchers during a game and Brother Matthias put George on the mound. Within minutes, George knew he had found his position.

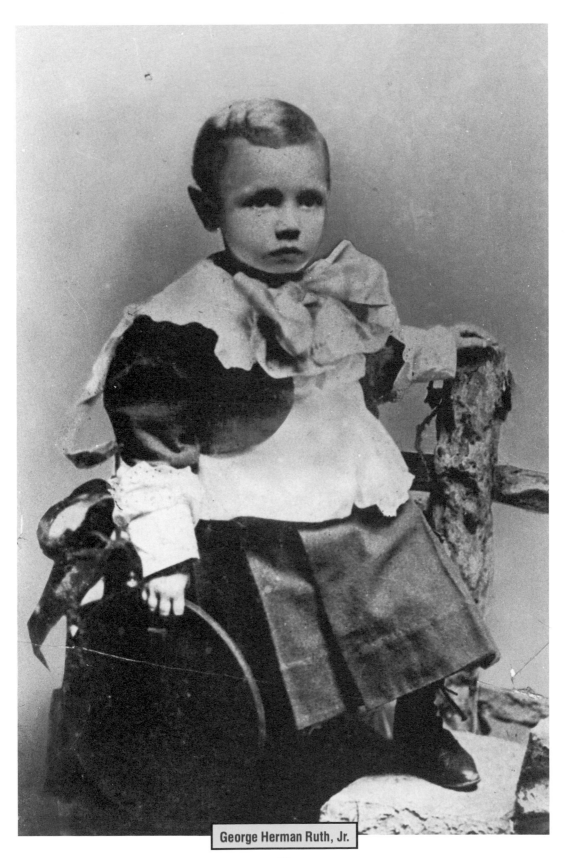

George Herman Ruth, Jr.

From then on, he was St. Mary's star pitcher.

When George turned 19, Brother Matthias introduced him to Jack Dunn, owner of the Baltimore Orioles baseball team of the International League. Dunn offered George a contract to play for the Orioles.

Suddenly, the "incorrigible" boy from the docks was going to be earning $600 a year playing baseball! When he left St. Mary's with Jack Dunn in late February of 1914, it was for the last time.

George's youth and enthusiasm made him stand out among the older, more experienced players on his team. During his first month with the Orioles, the other players started calling him "Babe." The nickname stuck. From then on, George Herman Ruth would be known as Babe Ruth.

Babe pitched less than a year for the Orioles' minor league team before he was sold to the Boston Red Sox of the American League. He quickly became one of the best pitchers in the league. In the World Series of 1916 and 1918, Babe won all three of the games he pitched for the Red Sox. At one point, he held his opponents scoreless for 29⅔ innings, a Series record that stood for 43 years!

In 1919, two events changed the Babe's life forever. In the early part of the season, Boston manager Ed Barrow asked Babe whether he preferred to pitch or hit. Babe answered that he would like to hit more often, so he was moved from the pitching rotation to the outfield. Suddenly, he began to hit more home runs than anyone had ever hit before.

Also in 1919, the most terrible scandal in baseball history rocked the game. In the World Series the heavily favored Chicago White Sox lost to the Cincinnati Reds. Rumors spread that several of the Sox's best players had been paid by gamblers to lose on purpose. The eight players involved were suspended from baseball and eventually barred from the sport for life. This betrayal outraged baseball fans.

The new Commissioner of Baseball, Judge Kenesaw Mountain Landis, had been debating whether to use a new, "livelier" baseball. Batters would be able to hit the new ball much farther than the old one. (Home runs in those days were not an everyday occurrence.)

The Chicago "Black Sox," as they were known forever afterward, had tarnished baseball's image, and Landis knew that he needed something to bring fans back to the ballpark. Young Babe Ruth was already hitting long balls and thrilling the fans who saw him. Landis decided to help Babe along and approved the use of the livelier baseball.

Babe had hit a record 29 homers in 1919. But after the introduction of the lively ball, Babe *really* began to hit home runs. In 1920, after his contract was sold to the New York Yankees, he hit 54!

Babe Ruth was an instant celebrity in New York. He lived his life in grand style, earning thousands of dollars a year, eating and drinking at a tremendous pace, staying in the most lavish hotels. He was also a friendly, outgoing man who enjoyed being around people, particularly children. He always had time to autograph a baseball for a young fan, and he often visited children in hospitals to cheer them up.

With one child, he did more than cheer him up. The boy was lying in a hospital bed, critically ill, when Babe visited him. Babe told the boy he would hit a home

The 1919 Chicago White Sox became known as the "Black Sox" when some of the players accepted money to lose the World Series.

run especially for him. He did, and against all odds the boy made a full recovery!

For all these reasons, Babe Ruth was the kind of larger-than-life hero baseball had been waiting for. On the field, he slugged 714 lifetime home runs, a record that stood for almost 40 years. Off the field, he was a world-famous celebrity who was always the center of attention.

When he was a child, he had never received enough warmth or love from his family. But later in life, Babe Ruth became the best-loved player in the history of baseball.

BABE RUTH'S CAREER HIGHLIGHTS:

- **Lifetime home runs—714 (record broken by Hank Aaron, 1974).**
- **Lifetime batting average—.342.**
- **One of the first five players named to the Baseball Hall of Fame, 1936.**

Lou Gehrig was called "The Iron Horse" because he never missed a single game in 13 ½ years.

NEW YORK BOY

He was born and raised in New York City and died there, and his life would certainly have been different had he grown up anywhere else. Some boys are shaped mainly by the influence of their families and their home environments. Though his parents' love and belief in him were a great influence, Lou Gehrig was largely shaped by the city of his childhood.

Lou had never left New York until the end of high school. In June of 1920, he made his first trip away from home. He and his coach and teammates from the High School of Commerce traveled to Chicago to play an inter-city baseball championship game against Chicago's Lane Technical High School. For 17-year-old Lou, it seemed the most glamorous experience possible. The boys would be playing at Wrigley Field, home of the Chicago Cubs. And that wasn't even the exciting part!

Imagine sleeping in a Pullman car! Imagine eating in a fancy dining car as your train speeds along in the night! The boys were even more impressed when the former President of the United States, William Howard Taft, who was also riding on the train, came in to visit with them and to wish them luck.

Lou and his teammates were amazed at the size of the hotel lobby in Chicago and a little overwhelmed by all the types of food listed on the menus they were handed in the restaurant. On the playing field, though, they got right down to business.

Lane Tech took an early four-run lead when the New York boys ran into two problems. First, pitcher Eli Jacobs, usually a tough and daring pitcher, could not settle his nerves. In the early innings, he threw a number of wild pitches. When he did succeed in putting the ball over the plate, the Chicago batters hit almost everything he threw.

To make matters worse, catcher Al McLaughlin injured his left ankle when he was running back to catch a foul ball. As the innings went on, his ankle swelled up and soon McLaughlin was hobbling more than walking.

Coach Harry Kane had brought only nine boys with him. He had no substitutes on the bench for either Jacobs or McLaughlin, so they had to stay in the game if Commerce intended to keep playing.

By the eighth inning, the score was tied, 8–8. In the ninth, with the bases loaded, Lou stepped up to the plate. Kane was convinced he knew what was going to happen.

He was right. Lou liked the first pitch, swung powerfully and connected. The ball soared over the rightfield fence, scoring four runs. It was a huge wallop in a major league stadium for a boy still in high school. Even the Chicago fans were cheering as Lou rounded the bases.

More important to Lou than the cheers at the game was the reception at the train station in New York when he and the Commerce team returned home. As the train from Chicago pulled into the station, the team was met with cheers from hundreds of students. Almost the entire Commerce student body had come down to the station to scream their approval for Lou. His schoolmates were so thrilled that they picked Lou up and carried him on their shoulders out of the station. They jammed into taxis and headed for school, where they crowded into the school auditorium and continued to cheer Lou and the team for several hours.

Though the Chicago newspapers had spoken of him with wonder, calling him the next Babe Ruth, this approval from his friends and classmates meant more to Lou than anything. If New York loved what he had done, then he must have done all right.

New York always fascinated the son of Henry and Christina Gehrig. Henry Louis Gehrig was born in the big city on June 19, 1903, at his parents' small home on East 94th Street. Three other children were also born to the Gehrigs, but each died in infancy. Only Lou survived.

His parents were quiet, hard-working German immigrants. Mr. Gehrig worked as a laborer in a wrought iron foundry, where the hours were long and the pay was poor. The family had to move several times in order to find homes where they could afford the monthly rent. The Gehrigs finally settled in a house on Amsterdam Avenue, only a few streets away from Hilltop Park, home of New York's American League team. Though the team was called the Highlanders in those days, it would soon become the Yankees.

Lou loved the sights and sounds of New York. He especially enjoyed watching the lights on the great bridges spanning the city. He wanted to be an engineer when he grew up so he could build great bridges, too. His parents were proud of his ambition. They wanted him to go to college and learn as much as he could.

In his early years, Lou, like so many other New York kids, spent much of his spare time in the sandlots, playing baseball in the spring and football in the fall. In the winter, his father took him to a gymnasium where Lou learned to work on the parallel bars, the wooden horse and the tumbling mats. He became an excellent young gymnast. In the summer he even swam in the Hudson River!

For all his enthusiasm for sports, Lou was not naturally gifted at athletics. He had to work harder to play as well as some of his friends. He was patient, though, and hard work did come naturally to him.

Lou was very young when his father became ill. The years at the iron foundry had destroyed Mr. Gehrig's health. Soon he had to spend most of his time in bed, saving his strength.

Lou considered it his duty to pitch in. He wanted to quit school and work full time, but his mother wouldn't allow it. She wanted Lou to go to college, so she went to work herself, cooking, cleaning and sewing for other people. Lou helped her before he left for school in the morning and after school before he sat down to do his homework.

Mrs. Gehrig managed to find time to cook and clean for her own family as well, and often prepared Lou's favorite dish, pickled eels. As he grew older, Lou was convinced that the eels were the reason for his strength and skill as a ballplayer. He even tried to persuade his teammates to try them!

By the time Lou entered the High School of Commerce, his father had become well enough to join his mother at work. They took jobs at the Sigma Nu fraternity house at Columbia University, one of New York's great colleges. His mother was a cook, his father, the handyman.

When he could, Lou helped cook breakfast at the fraternity house, waited tables at dinner and washed dishes afterward. The boys in the fraternity liked him. He was hard-working and uncomplaining. They called him "The Little Dutch Boy" because of his crisp, clipped hairstyle, and invited him to play baseball with them in his spare time.

At Commerce, Lou became an athletic star. His diligence made him an excellent baseball player. He played several positions—first base, outfield and pitcher—and was the team's best hitter. He was also a talented fullback on the football team, played soccer and continued his gymnastics. On one remarkable day in the fall of 1920, Lou had two very different athletic triumphs. In the morning, he kicked the winning goal in a soccer game, and that afternoon he threw the winning touchdown pass for the football team!

Lou never forgot his parents' desire to see him go to college. By the time he became a senior at Commerce, his athletic ability was so impressive that 24 different colleges had invited Lou to enroll. But Lou hoped to remain in New York.

One day in his senior year at Commerce, Lou starred in a football game on South Field, which was part of Columbia University. A Columbia graduate named Robert W. Watt, who was the graduate manager of athletics at Columbia, attended the game and was impressed with Lou.

Bobby Watt had been one of the leading members of the Sigma Nu fraternity house during the years that the Gehrigs had worked there. In fact, he had been the person who hired them. Now, looking at the beefy young man in the Commerce uniform, he didn't realize he was looking at "The Little Dutch Boy." Lou had grown so tall and husky that Watt didn't recognize him!

When Lou's parents greeted Watt and pointed out their son, Bobby eagerly signed him up for Columbia. He knew that Lou would be a star on the football team. What he didn't know was that Lou also played baseball.

Columbia soon found out all about Lou's baseball talents. When he asked in his usual modest way if he could just work out with the freshman team, the coaches immediately saw his amazing talent and power. They told him to forget about the freshman team and sent him straight to the varsity.

In 1922, the New York Yankees sent a scout to watch Lou in a game. He stepped to the plate in the ninth inning and broke a 2–2 tie with a home run that soared out of the field and across the street to the steps of the library. It was one of the longest hits anyone had ever seen at Columbia. The Yankees signed him right away.

Henry Louis Gehrig wanted to be an engineer when he grew up.

For two years, Lou played in the minors with brief appearances for the Yankees. In 1925 he stuck with the big club. On June 1, he pinch-hit and played rightfield. The next day, he took over at first base. For the next 13½ years, Lou would play every day. He ran up a string of 2,130 consecutive games—a record that has never been approached. For his extraordinary endurance, he was nicknamed "The Iron Horse." He was one of New York's best-loved players, the captain of the team and the man known as "The Pride of the Yankees."

But by 1938 it was apparent that something was wrong with Lou. He could not play as well as he had always played. He consulted with doctors at the Mayo Clinic in Minnesota, who told him what was wrong.

In the spring of 1939, Lou Gehrig took himself out of the Yankees lineup. He may not have realized it, but he was dying. Lou had amyotrophic [*ay-my-oh-TROF-ic*] lateral sclerosis [*skler-O-sis*], or ALS, a disease that attacks and weakens the muscles. Eventually patients with ALS become so weak they can't even button their shirts or tie their shoelaces.

On July 4, 1939, the Yankees held a Lou Gehrig Appreciation Day at Yankee Stadium. Thousands of fans turned out to cheer him. Between games of a doubleheader, Yankees players and officials stepped to the microphone at home plate to praise and honor him. Finally it was Lou's turn to speak.

A hush fell over the stadium as he stepped to the microphone. "I consider myself the luckiest man on the face of the earth," he said. "I may have had a tough bad break, but I have an awful lot to live for," he said.

Lou spent the remainder of the 1939 season at Yankee Stadium, watching the Yankees win the pennant and then the World Series in four straight games. He still felt like a Yankee, even if he couldn't join his teammates on the field.

Mayor Fiorello LaGuardia offered Lou a position on the New York City Parole Board, helping young men who had gone wrong to straighten out their lives. Lou eagerly accepted the job. He loved the idea of helping out the boys of New York, for he knew what it meant to be a New York boy himself.

On June 2, 1941, a few weeks before his 38th birthday, Lou died at home. The next day Mayor LaGuardia ordered flags flown at half-mast, a gesture usually reserved for the deaths of presidents and heads of state. However, Lou Gehrig was an unusual man. And a New York boy to the end.

LOU GEHRIG'S CAREER HIGHLIGHTS:

- **Hit 23 grand slam home runs, a major league record.**
- **Played in 2,130 consecutive ball games (June 1, 1925 to May 1, 1939), a major league record.**
- **Highest batting average for one year—.379 in 1930.**
- **Inducted into the Hall of Fame, 1939.**

Ty Cobb was a fierce competitor all his life.

THE SOUTHERN TORNADO

Roylston, Georgia, in 1897 was a small, rural town. The soft-spoken residents were devoted to their families, worked faithfully at their jobs and attended church every Sunday. Many of them came from families which had lived in Roylston for several generations.

But all was not quiet in Roylston. The children, for instance, were often restless in school. Like children everywhere, they were more interested in pulling hair, squirting ink out of inkwells and playing games in the schoolyard than they were in their lessons.

One day, the fifth-grade class divided into teams for a spelling bee. The boys were on one team, the girls on the other. Both teams had worked hard preparing for the spelling bee and now they would see which side was better.

The teacher began to call out the words to be spelled. One by one, a member of each team stepped forward, spelled the word and stepped back into line. When a word was misspelled, the contestant had to leave the team. The last team with a player left would win the spelling bee.

One of the boys was even more driven to win the bee than his teammates were. He was Tyrus Raymond Cobb, son of the mayor of Roylston who was also the local newspaper editor. Ty was always fiercely competitive, both in the schoolroom and on the playing fields. Now he wanted his team to win the spelling bee.

The boys' team was down to its last player. Ty himself had been eliminated, but he and the other boys hoped their one remaining teammate would be able to beat the girls' team.

The teacher gave the boy a word to spell. He hesitated for a moment, then slowly began to spell it out. The teacher shook her head. He had spelled it wrong and the girls' team had won the spelling bee.

The other boys were disappointed at losing to the girls, but they soon forgot about it. Ty did not. After school, he waited for the boy who had spelled the last word wrong. Ty pounced on him and beat him up. From Ty's point of view, the boy hadn't worked hard enough to prepare himself for the spelling bee and he had hurt his team by being careless. Ty's own behavior was inexcusable, but Ty couldn't stand losing. This drive to excel was the force behind one of baseball's most dominant players. Because he was so ruthlessly driven, he was hard on other people and few ever really liked him.

Ty Cobb was the oldest of three children, two sons and a daughter, born to William Herschel Cobb and Amanda Chitwood Cobb. W.H. was a dignified, well-read young schoolteacher of 20 when he married Amanda, the daughter of the wealthiest family in northern Banks County, Georgia. She was only 12 years old at the time!

Three years later, on December 18, 1886, in Narrows, Georgia, Amanda gave birth to her first son. Her husband read about the siege of the city of Tyre in the fourth century B.C. and admired Tyre's stubborn refusal to yield to the armies of Alexander the Great. W.H. decided to name his son Tyrus in honor of the ancient Phoenician city.

His father's influence was the force that shaped Ty Cobb's life. W.H. Cobb believed strongly in the power of education to uplift and change people. Starting out as a rural schoolmaster, he had worked his way up to become editor of the Roylston newspaper and mayor of the town. Eventually, he was even elected to the state senate.

W.H. was respected and admired by the townspeople. He wanted his children to earn respect and admiration as well and encouraged them to learn and to work hard. He was especially proud of Ty, who showed early signs of intelligence. In school, Ty did well in grammar and arithmetic and took a couple of prizes for speechmaking. This encouraged his father, who hoped Ty would go to West Point or become a lawyer.

Ty loved his father and tried very hard to make W.H. proud of him. His friends noticed that Ty always drove himself hard and competed fiercely with others. He often became angry with schoolmates who weren't as determined as he was to win. He seemed to think faster and move more quickly than other boys his age. No matter how good he was at something, though, he always pushed himself to do better.

But Ty's real interests did not lie in the schoolroom. Unlike W.H., Ty was more attracted to athletic contests than to intellectual competition. He ran races with his friends, climbed trees, even walked a tightrope stretched high over the street in the middle of town.

Ty also began to play baseball. With his intelligence, speed and physical daring, he was a natural.

Roylston's young players formed a team called the Rompers and Ty played with them until he was 14. The older players, including many grown men, played on a team called the Reds. When the Reds found themselves without a shortstop one day, they asked Ty to fill in. The boy, though younger and smaller than the other players, successfully handled eight plays at shortstop without an error and hit safely three times.

Soon Ty was focusing all his considerable energy on baseball. At 14, he sewed together his own glove and ordered pamphlets on sprinting to improve his base-running skills. After he joined the Reds on a regular basis, he quickly became their star. This angered his father, who saw all his careful plans for Ty going up in smoke.

Tyrus Raymond Cobb.

He thought Ty was wasting his time playing a silly game when he should have been preparing himself for an important career. Ty was torn between his love for baseball and his love for his father. He still desperately wanted his father's approval.

But Ty knew he had no interest in studying the law. He just wanted to play professional baseball for any team that would take him, and he wanted his father's blessing for the life he had chosen.

Ty finally left home in 1904, at the age of 17, to try out with a minor league team. His father told him simply, "Don't come home a failure." Ty considered those words the most inspirational he had ever heard, though he felt that W.H. was not happy with his decision to become a ballplayer. Ty still craved his father's approval and hoped to earn it. That season, he played for a team in Augusta, Georgia, and one in Anniston, Alabama.

The following year, his season was interrupted by a telegram which told him to come home at once. His father had died in a shooting accident.

Ty hurried home to find even worse news waiting for him. His father had been killed by two shotgun blasts fired by Ty's mother, Amanda. W.H. had come home late at night and in the darkness Amanda had mistaken him for a burglar. She was arrested for manslaughter. Ty was devastated. He had hoped he and his father would someday grow closer. Now they never would. The unspoken feelings he had for his father would haunt him the rest of his life.

Ty spent four days at home with his family and then returned to his ball club. He reasoned that his last duty to his dead father was to uphold his family's reputation and the best way to do that was to become a great ballplayer.

Later that season, the Detroit Tigers spotted Ty and offered him a spot as an outfielder on their major league roster. Ty accepted eagerly. He was on his way.

Ty's boyhood drive to succeed became even more ferocious after his father's death. Winning was all important to the talented young player. While he was not as fast as some players or as powerful as others, Ty spent his major league career outthinking the competition.

As a Detroit Tiger, he was such a vicious competitor that many people, even his own teammates, hated him. His favorite trick was to slide into a stolen base with his feet held high. The spikes on the soles of his baseball shoes prevented most fielders from coming close enough to tag him out. Those who insisted on trying to make the tag found their arms and legs ripped open by the spikes.

But Ty Cobb was also a man who gave his whole heart to the game. He played day in and day out, even when he was ill or in pain from injuries. Once, three men jumped him on a dark night, and slashed him in the back with a knife. Ty chased them, catching and beating two very badly. The next day, with a bandage over the wound, he played as though nothing had happened.

Another time, his doctor insisted he take a three-day rest because he had a high temperature and his legs were swollen and raw. Ty paid no attention. In a game that afternoon, he had three hits and stole three bases, sliding into the bag each time on his battered legs in defiance of both the pain and the doctor.

Toward the end his brilliant 24-year playing career, Ty managed the Tigers for five seasons. His philosophy as a manager was exactly the same as it had been when he was a player. He said, "I saw no point in losing if I could win."

When baseball's Hall of Fame was completed in Cooperstown, New York, in 1936, the very first memento chosen for the Hall was a pair of Ty's spiked shoes. He had indeed brought respect and honor to the family name. His father would have been proud.

TY COBB'S CAREER HIGHLIGHTS:

- **One of the first five players elected to the Hall of Fame, 1936.**
- **Lifetime hits—4,191 (record broken by Pete Rose, 1985).**
- **Lifetime average—.367 (a major league record).**
- **Career runs scored—2,245 (A major league record).**

SUPERSTARS FROM THE GLORY DAYS

2

As the Great Depression settled over America in the 1930s, baseball became even more important to the fans, who needed something to think about besides finding a job and keeping food on the table. Watching their favorite teams play was the ideal diversion.

Game tickets cost very little. But even if you couldn't afford a quarter for a bleacher seat, you could always listen to your team on the radio, the newest method of getting close to the action. Fans no longer had to wait for the next day's newspaper to check on what happened to their team.

As World War II drew closer, more and more stars began to emerge on the playing field. There were wonderful hitters like Ted Williams and Hank Greenberg. Colorful catchers like Ernie Lombardi and Mickey Cochrane added pizzazz to the game. And a fastball-throwing phenomenon named Bob Feller had everyone in the American League excited. It was a wonderful time to be a baseball fan.

Joe DiMaggio and later Mickey Mantle and Willie Mays caught the spirit of the times and created their own brand of excitement with their style of play. They were three of the most glorious players ever to walk onto a field. From the very first crack of their bats, they were hotshots.

As a teenager, Joe DiMaggio (right) played for the San Francisco Seals in the Pacific Coast League.

GLIDING TO A RECORD

There is a certain beauty to coming from a large, bustling family. There may not always be enough new pants to go around, but there is always lots of advice. For a lucky younger brother that could mean lots of help and instruction from older brothers who know the ways of the world and, most importantly, the ways of sports. Joe DiMaggio was such a lucky younger brother.

Joseph Paul DiMaggio was born in Martinez, California, on November 25, 1914, the eighth in a family of nine children. When he was very young, the family moved to the North Beach section of San Francisco, near the docks. Joe's father, Giuseppe, had come from Sicily to America in 1902 with his wife and baby daughter. Like so many immigrants, they were looking for a better life. Giuseppe changed his name to Joseph, the English version of Giuseppe. He was a hard-working man who hoped his sons would work with him on his fishing boat when they grew up.

Money was often hard to come by in the DiMaggio household. In those days it cost 25 cents to see a movie. Thirteen-year-old Joe, Jr. had eagerly looked forward to seeing Al Jolson in *The Jazz Singer,* the first full-length talking movie, at the local theater. But when the movie came to North Beach, there wasn't a spare quarter to be found for a trip to the theater. Joe was disappointed, but he knew that keeping the family fed was far more important than going to the movies.

In the DiMaggio household there was always plenty of good food, especially the fish that Joseph, Sr. brought home from his daily catch. Joe's mother Rosalie spoke very little English, but her spicy Italian cooking always drew friends in for a meal. Later, the family opened a seafood restaurant in San Francisco that featured many of Rosalie's specialties.

The DiMaggio sons all seemed to have their sights on baseball. Tom was the best player in the family. But since he was the oldest son, it was his responsibility to help his father. Eventually, he gave up baseball altogether in order to go into the family fishing business.

Joe, the fourth son, couldn't stand the thought of being a fisherman. To begin with, he hated the smell of fish! He hated handling their slippery bodies. He didn't

23

even like being out on a boat. He helped out with chores around the house, but whenever he had a free moment, he spent it playing baseball with his brothers or with his friends at the local Boys' Club.

In his early teens, Joe learned how to play tennis. Though he still loved baseball, for a time he wondered if he should try playing professional tennis. He was developing a tall, lean body that was well-suited to that game. But the long solitary hours and endless drills did not suit his personality, and when Joe quit high school at 17, he left tennis behind. Joseph, Sr. was not pleased that his son had left school without graduating. He worried that young Joe would never get a steady job. But Joe was determined to help the family as a wage-earner and he took a job in an orange juice factory.

Joe's older brother Vince was already earning good money as a ballplayer. He played in the outfield for the San Francisco Seals in the Pacific Coast League, and could take home as much as $250 a month when he was playing full-time. In 1932, when Joe was 17, Vince arranged for him to play three games for the Seals at the end of the season as a fill-in shortstop. The next year, Joe was a full-time Seals outfielder. He had taken over the job from Vince, who was sent to a team in Hollywood for the season. Every major league team sent scouts to look at the younger DiMaggio, who was tearing up the Pacific Coast League in his first full year.

In addition to hitting for a high average, Joe really made the scouts sit up and take notice when he hit safely in 61 consecutive games. No one had ever done it before—and no one has done it since! Without his older brothers, however, Joe might not have had the chance.

Joseph, Sr. was distressed to see Joe and Vince becoming more and more involved in baseball. He believed that a man's work should be some form of hard labor and he felt that it was somehow wrong for his sons to be earning money playing a game.

But he had to face the fact that his sons were serious about spending their lives as ballplayers. Vince was already earning his living that way. When Joe approached his father with the same situation, Joseph, Sr. threw up his hands. He was disappointed in Joe's career choice, but he loved his son and wanted him to be happy. He could do nothing with his namesake but hug him and wish him luck.

By the time the 18-year-old Joe finished his first full season with the Seals in 1933, many scouts were asking what it would cost to buy his contract. Charles Graham, the owner of the Seals, was asking for $75,000, a huge amount of money at a time when a loaf of bread cost a nickel! The New York Yankees were interested, but they had hoped to get Joe for a lot less money.

In 1934, Joe went back to the Seals. One day in the middle of the season, he stepped off a crowded bus and popped his left knee. The pain almost made him collapse on the sidewalk. At the age of 19, he had suffered the first of a number of serious injuries. Most of his season was over.

Usually when a player gets hurt, scouts turn away because the player is considered a bad risk. Luckily, the Yankees chief scout knew Joe and knew how well he could play. When he heard of the injury, he recommended that the Yankees offer the Seals far less than $75,000. The Seals gave in. Encouraged by his brother Tom,

Joe eventually signed a contract to play for the Yankees for $8,000, which was an excellent salary for a rookie player. Joe spent one more year in the minors getting his left leg healthy.

Joe came to New York for the 1936 season. All the players had already heard of him. Joe was supposed to be the new hotshot! But during spring training, he was injured again when a heat lamp burned his foot during treatment for a sprained ankle. Joe missed opening day of his first season as a Yankee.

As soon as he was able to play again, Joe began to prove that the newspaper articles about his ability were not just hype. "Joltin' Joe" hit long balls and ran like a champion. His throwing arm was accurate and powerful. He moved so smoothly that the sportswriters nicknamed him "The Yankee Clipper," after the beautiful and graceful 19th-century sailing ships that once glided into the New York harbor.

Joe became an instant star in New York. Even more satisfying to him was his father's sudden transformation into an avid baseball fan. Joe loved the idea that his father read the box scores every day and criticized the official scorers if he thought they had made a mistake. His father was finally interested in the game Joe and his brothers had always loved.

"Joltin' Joe" takes a swing for the New York Yankees.

By 1941 Joe DiMaggio had become one of baseball's greatest stars. His batting average was always high, he hit for power and he fielded with speed and grace. On May 15, Joe hit a short single against the Chicago White Sox, the first hit of the longest consecutive-game hitting streak in major league history. As the weeks passed and Yankees fans held their breath, Joe continued to hit safely at least once in every single game he played.

He broke the Yankees club record, which stood at 29 games. He broke the American League record of 41 games. Finally, he busted the all-time record, which had been set in 1897, of 44 games. The attention became intense. How far could he go? And what team would finally end his streak?

The streak ended on July 17, when Joe failed to get a hit against the Cleveland Indians. By then he had hit safely in 56 consecutive games. His record still stands! It was his greatest achievement as a ballplayer.

Injuries continued to haunt Joe. As the years went by, he was plagued by a swollen neck, bad knees and torn muscles in his lower legs. Mysterious fevers often sent him to bed. And he once had an operation for bone spurs in his heels, a condition where chips of bone interfere with the normal working of the heel. Each injury seemed to take him off the playing field for a long period of time.

In December of 1951, Joe announced that he was leaving baseball. Though he was only 37, Joe had been worn down by the long string of injuries. He wanted people to remember him at his best, and if he couldn't be the "Yankee Clipper" of the early years, he didn't want to play at all.

A few years after his retirement from baseball, he married beautiful movie star Marilyn Monroe. Marilyn was popular around the world and, like many screen stars, she made special trips overseas to entertain American soldiers. When she returned from one trip to Korea, she told Joe excitedly, "Oh, Joe, it was wonderful. You never heard such cheering!"

Joe just smiled, thinking back on his playing days, and answered softly, "Yes, I have."

JOE DIMAGGIO'S CAREER HIGHLIGHTS:

- **American League Most Valuable Player, 1939, 1941 and 1947.**
- **Longest consecutive-game hitting streak—56 games, 1941 (a major league record).**
- **Won AL batting title, 1939 and 1940.**
- **Won AL home run crown, 1937 and 1948.**
- **Inducted into the Hall of Fame, 1955.**

BORN TO BE A SUPERSTAR

It was tough being a lead and zinc miner in Spavinaw, Oklahoma, especially in the early days of the Great Depression. Elvin Mantle, nicknamed "Mutt" by his friends, knew just how tough it was because he'd been a miner all his life. It was a difficult job and it hardly paid enough to feed and shelter him and his wife, Lovell. As he sat with his father in their small, dim kitchen on the day in October of 1931 when his wife was to have a baby, Mutt vowed his child would have a better life than he had had.

After hours of waiting, Mutt heard the cry of a newborn infant from the bedroom. When the doctor came out of the room a few minutes later, he confirmed what Mutt had been sure of for months: He had a son.

Mutt had already determined how to help his son achieve a better life. Mutt and his father were passionate baseball fans. Though they spent their lives working for their families, their dreams and pleasures focused completely on baseball. When they were together, the two talked constantly about baseball.

Mutt was a good player. In what spare time he had, he played a little with just about every team in Oklahoma that needed an extra player. He devoured sports magazines and newspapers.

Mutt believed that a boy who grew up to play professional baseball would have a fine future. He vowed to devote as much time, experience and money as possible to turn his child into the best baseball player possible. That way, he reasoned, his child would have a marketable skill with which he could earn a good living.

Mutt had already made up his mind about the child's name. He figured a boy with a ballplayer's name would grow up to be a ballplayer. He reluctantly agreed that his son's middle name would be Charles, after his and Lovell's fathers. The first name, however, Mutt insisted was to be Mickey, after Mickey Cochrane, the star catcher of the Philadelphia Athletics. The child was named Mickey Charles Mantle.

Mutt did not even wait a full day after Mickey's birth before introducing him to baseball. Leaning over the cradle, Mutt held a baseball above the cooing baby. "Get a good look at it, Sonny," he told the infant. "You'll be seeing a lot more!"

Mickey Mantle had a spectacular 17-year career in the major leagues.

Within a few days Mutt had filled the cradle with baseballs, as a good-luck symbol for little Mickey. Lovell finally had to tell him to remove some of the balls, because there wasn't enough room left for the baby. Mutt spent every minute of his spare time at the cradle, where he talked to Mickey about baseball. He wanted his son to learn all about the game as early as possible.

When he was three, Mickey learned to count by listening to his father count off the number of bases on a baseball diamond. Just for fun, Mutt began throwing a small rubber ball at Mickey. Mutt gave Mickey a little stick and told him to tap the ball with the stick. He was thrilled to see that little Mickey was already well-coordinated.

By six, when Mickey was big enough to start playing with a real baseball, he already had a real, major league-style uniform. His father had cut up his own precious uniform to make one for his son.

Now the lessons began in earnest. Mutt didn't just want Mickey to hit well. He reasoned that the boy would go further if he was a natural switch-hitter, someone who could hit powerfully from either the left or the right side of the plate. Mutt spent hours every day working with Mickey and showing him how to stand, how to swing, how to run.

Baseball bound father and son together; they were together every free moment Mutt could spare. It was Mutt's way of showing Mickey how much he loved him. Mickey appreciated how his father talked to him about the game. His father never treated him like a child. Mutt always talked to Mickey as an adult. Mutt always explained that he was teaching Mickey to play baseball so that Mickey's life would be better than his own.

Mutt's influence on Mickey was very strong. When Mickey began to play for the Douhat team in Oklahoma's Pee-Wee League, he chose to be a catcher, the position played by Mutt's idol, Mickey Cochrane. However, the lessons his father taught him about recognizing and using his ability soon helped him realize that catching wasn't his best position.

By the age of 11, Mickey was already one of the fastest runners in his league. He could speed down to first base or dash home in a blur of dust. Squatting behind the plate wasn't helping his legs or giving him a chance to use all of his abilities. When Mickey asked his coach to move him to second base, where he could better use his speed, Mutt was proud of him for thinking for himself.

As Mickey reached high-school age, he began to play football. He loved the game and enjoyed his position as Commerce High School's star halfback. His coach valued Mickey's amazing speed on the field. Once he had the ball, no one was fast enough to stop him!

During one school football game, another player kicked the 15-year-old Mickey in the ankle. At first, he thought nothing of it. But by the next morning, his ankle was swollen to twice its normal size and had turned almost black! Mutt rushed Mickey to the doctor who determined that Mickey had osteomyelitis (os-tee-oh-my-uh-*LITE*-is), a serious bone infection. Mickey needed hospital treatment as quickly as possible.

Mickey spent several weeks in the hospital, certain that he would be well when he left. When he was being discharged, however, his doctor handed him a pair of crutches and told him he would never play ball again! His illness was so serious he was lucky to be able to use his legs at all.

Mickey could hardly believe what the doctor had said, but he soon realized it was true. On some days, he felt fine and he could go out and throw a baseball or run the bases with no problems. On other days, he was in such pain that he couldn't stand up.

Mutt kept his worries to himself. He encouraged Mickey, assuring him that baseball wasn't the only thing in life. But Mickey was depressed. He couldn't imagine life without baseball.

One day, to cheer Mickey up, Mutt dug into his savings and bought tickets to a Cardinals game in St. Louis. Mickey loved watching the pros dashing around the field. His smile grew brighter as the innings went by.

Mutt was delighted. He had hoped that seeing others who could play the game wouldn't upset Mickey or remind him of his own problem. It seemed to help the boy to forget his own troubles for a while.

Mutt was wrong. Mickey hadn't forgotten. When the game ended, he turned to his father and said determinedly, "Dad, give those crutches away today. I won't need them anymore. My sideline days are over."

He was right. No illness was going to stop Mutt Mantle's son. Mickey returned to baseball and football, and even went out for the basketball team. Though he visited the doctor every week and endured daily treatments at home on his leg, Mickey refused to give up sports. He was going to play as long as his legs would hold him up.

At 16, Mickey was playing shortstop in the Ban Johnson League, an organized amateur league. A friend of Mutt's spotted Mickey and invited him to join a team in Baxter Springs, Oklahoma. Then an umpire who saw Mickey play on the Baxter Springs team suggested he try out for the Yankees farm club. Mickey was on his way!

The Yankees assigned him to play Class D ball in Independence, Missouri, during the 1949 season. A year later, he moved up to Class C ball in Joplin, Missouri. The following year, at 19, Mickey went to the major leagues as a New York Yankee!

It might seem by this time that Mickey had outgrown his need for his father. After all, now he had major league coaches and players to teach him the fine points of his game. His father's counsel might get in the way of the professional advice.

Nothing could have been further from the truth. Mutt made the long trip to New York to see Mickey play in his first major league game, and Mutt was the proudest person in the park. At mid-season, Mickey suddenly found himself confused by major league pitching. Mickey couldn't seem to hit the way he always had. The Yankees sent him down to their minor league team in Kansas City. A week or so later, Mutt visited his son to see if he could help.

In his first 10 games with the Kansas City team, Mickey didn't get a single hit. He was very upset with himself. He had spent his entire life preparing for a career in baseball, and now, at 19, he felt he was washed up. He wondered whether he had chosen the wrong career.

Mutt listened to his son one night as Mickey poured out his fears. He knew Mickey needed to get his confidence back before he could start hitting again. For

Mickey Charles Mantle, shown here as a youg man, was named for Mickey Cochrane, the star catcher for the Philadelphia Athletics.

the first time in his life, Mutt spoke harshly to Mickey. He reminded him that he was facing big league pitching now, and that baseball wouldn't be as easy for him as it had been before. Mutt told Mickey he couldn't quit unless he'd really given his best to the game. If he still couldn't cut it, then it was all right to say so. But no one at the age of 19 could know for sure that he was washed up!

Mickey listened. As always, his father knew exactly how to handle him. Mickey started hitting again and his confidence soared. A mere six weeks after he had been sent to Kansas City, the Yankees called him back to New York.

Mutt watched from the stands as Mickey and his teammates won the American League pennant in 1951. Mutt then saw Mickey play in his first World Series. Although Mickey was injured in the second game and had to sit out the rest of the Series, it was the biggest thrill of Mutt's life. The dreams he had held for his son since the night Mickey was born were coming true. Mutt's boy was becoming a major league star!

Having recovered from his injury, Mickey looked forward to an even better season in 1952. What he didn't know was that his father was dying of Hodgkin's disease. As always, though, Mutt thought only of his son and his son's baseball career. "Don't tell Mickey," he told his wife. "It might hurt his play if he knew."

One day at the beginning of the 1952 season, Mickey learned that his father was dead. It was a terrible blow. Mutt had been as important to Mickey's success in baseball as his own skill and talent had been. Mickey couldn't imagine playing baseball without his father watching and encouraging him from the sidelines.

But Mickey went on to have a spectacular 17-year career in the major leagues. He replaced the legendary Joe DiMaggio in centerfield and captivated the fans with his speed, his throwing accuracy and his powerful hitting. In April of 1953, he hit the longest measured home run in major league history, a 565-foot blast over the leftfield bleachers at Griffith Stadium in Washington, D.C. He is still considered baseball's greatest switch-hitter ever and was a hero for a generation of baseball fans.

Mickey was injured often during his career and frequently played in pain. Sometimes he was tempted to ease up a little and not work so hard. When that thought crossed his mind, though, he knew it was impossible. That's not how his father had taught him to play baseball.

MICKEY MANTLE'S CAREER HIGHLIGHTS:

- **Inducted into the Hall of Fame, 1974.**
- **Yankees uniform number (#7) retired, 1969.**
- **Total home runs—536.**
- **American League Most Valuable Player, 1956, 1957 and 1962.**
- **Won the AL Triple Crown, 1956—highest average (.353), most home runs (52), most RBIs (130). He is one of only 14 players to win a Triple Crown.**

LESSONS FROM CAT

There are times when every father has to teach his son important lessons. For William Howard Mays, one of those times came when his son Willie was 12. William had found Willie near their house in Fairfield, Alabama, sharing a bottle of liquor and smoking a cigarette with a friend. The boys thought these forbidden activities were cool. So William decided to teach Willie a thing or two about drinking and smoking.

He took Willie home and, when they were alone, he poured a glass of Old Crow, a popular whiskey. "You want to drink, Willie? Go ahead. Drink."

Willie wanted to say no, but he knew he couldn't. His father wanted to prove a point and Willie knew he had better obey. He lifted the glass and took a big gulp. The whiskey tasted like liquid fire and soon Willie was choking. His father invited him to finish up. Willie shook his head. He'd had enough.

Next William lit a big White Owl cigar. "You want to smoke, Willie? Here you go. Smoke."

The cigar was even worse than the whiskey. He tried one puff, but the tobacco was so harsh that it burned his throat and his nose. Sweat poured from his forehead. Willie felt sick and thought his eyes would never stop watering. With his father's permission, he crushed out the cigar in an ashtray.

Willie was never again tempted to hurt himself by drinking or smoking. It was a valuable lesson—especially valuable for a boy who would grow up to be one of baseball's greatest players.

Like Mutt Mantle, William Howard Mays cherished the idea of teaching his boy to play baseball. He had played in the Industrial League, an amateur league made up of players who worked in the mills around Birmingham. William was fast on his feet and his ability to snag a fly ball was uncanny. The other players called him "Cat." Unlike Mutt, however, he did not intend to push his son into a baseball career unless Willie showed an interest.

William and his wife, Ann, were both 18 years old when their son, Willie Howard Mays, Jr. was born on May 6, 1931, in the town of Westfield, Alabama, a suburb

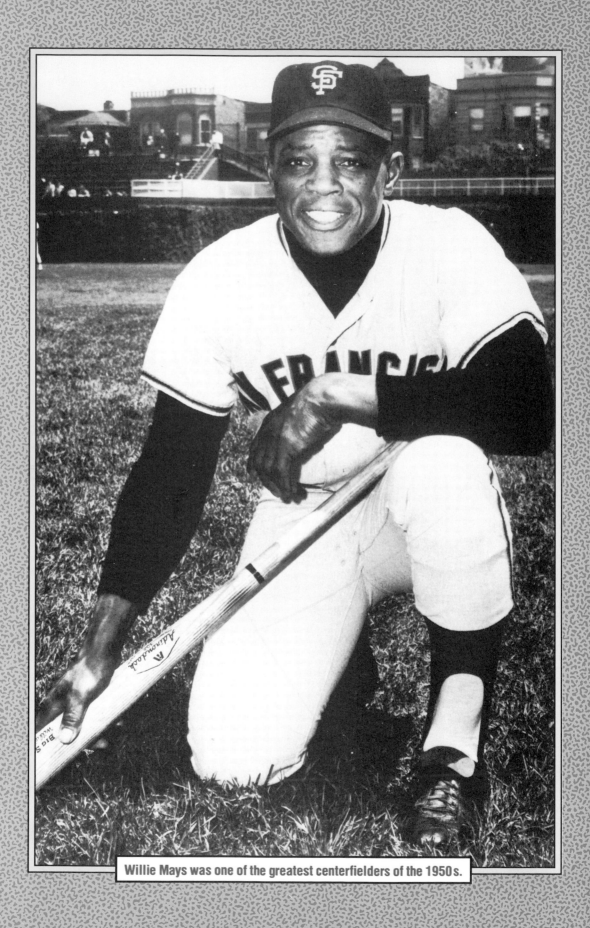

Willie Mays was one of the greatest centerfielders of the 1950s.

of the large industrial city of Birmingham. At the time, William was a porter on the train from Birmingham to Detroit and spent a lot of time away from home.

When he was at home, William focused on his son. Willie was only six months old when he began to walk and William thought it was the right time to begin teaching him about baseball. He pulled two chairs close together. Little Willie clung to one chair to keep his balance and William set a baseball on top of the other.

"See the ball, Willie," he told his son. "See the ball." Willie would toddle toward the baseball and try to grasp it in his little hands. He soon progressed to hitting a rubber ball across a room with a little stick and then crawling after it to hit it again.

William's absences from home hurt his marriage and he and Ann divorced when Willie was three years old. Ann married another man, with whom she had 10 more children. Willie lived with his father who raised the child himself.

Theirs was an unusual household. William took in two neighborhood kids who were orphaned when their parents died in an accident. Sarah and Ernestine shared household responsibilities and helped to support this makeshift family. There was also "Uncle" Otis Brooks, a friend of William's who lived with them and helped out with the chores.

William knew that he couldn't raise his son properly if he was spending most of his time on the road. He left his job with the railroad and took a position in the toolroom of a steel mill in Birmingham.

It was a happy life for Willie, although he hated doing chores around the house, and Sarah insisted he wash dishes, chop firewood and clean up the yard. But Otis usually did most of his chores for him, giving Willie extra time to play with his friends or throw a ball with his father. Ernestine gave Willie lunch money, usually $10 for a week's worth of lunches. What Ernestine didn't know was that Willie liked to share what he had with his friends. Instead of keeping the money for himself, he usually invited his pals to eat with him and his lunch money never lasted long!

When Willie was 10, his extended family moved out of Westfield to a town called Fairfield, a few miles away. Their neighborhood, nicknamed "The Heights," was where Willie first began to play games with other boys, both black and white.

Though there was still some segregation (separation of blacks and whites) in the South then, Willie always remembered those games as happy events. The boys themselves never fought each other over being white or black, though some of their parents were horrified when they learned about the games. Often, these angry parents would call the police and Willie and his friends would be forced to break up the game. The 10-year-old realized that kids didn't notice or care very much about race. It was adults who really kicked up a fuss about it.

Willie's first sports injury occurred when he was 12, though it didn't happen while he was playing a game. Though he loved baseball best, Willie liked watching football and enjoyed the Saturday afternoon games that nearby Miles College played against its rivals. Because there was no extra money around for Willie to buy tickets to the games, he usually climbed a tree overlooking the football field and watched the older boys play from there.

One Saturday Willie got a little careless and fell out of the tree while watching the game. He didn't realize he had suffered a serious injury until later when Sarah

The young Willie Mays played minor league ball for the Minneapolis Millers.

asked him to move a bucket of coal. When Willie reached for it, pain shot straight up to his shoulder. He had broken his arm.

When the arm healed, Willie found that he had a strange new ability. He could throw harder with that right arm than anyone in the neighborhood!

Fourteen-year-old Willie impressed the manager of the semi-pro Gray Sox, who had seen him playing in the neighborhood games. The manager asked Willie to play shortstop. When Willie threw to first base, his right arm was so strong that the first baseman complained that his hand hurt after catching Willie's throws. Only Charlie Willis, who was Willie's friend and the team's catcher, could bear to catch a ball that Willie threw. So the manager moved Willie to the pitcher's mound.

William Mays promptly put a stop to that. He reasoned that a pitcher's arm was delicate and, because a pitcher wasn't trained to field or hit, he was useless if he had an arm injury. In an instant, his career could be over! William knew that Willie was aiming at a career in baseball. He wanted to give his son every chance to succeed so he insisted that Willie give up pitching. William trained him to be an outfielder instead.

Willie honed his baseball skills more every day. No one realized how naturally gifted he was until the summer he was 15, when he and his father played together in the Industrial League.

By now William was 33. He wasn't as fast as he had once been, and his reflexes weren't as sharp. His nickname, "Cat," no longer made much sense. He played left-field and Willie played center.

During William's final game in the league, a player on the opposing team hit a long ball to left centerfield. It was a ball William would have easily caught a few years before. Instead, he stood and watched with wonder as his son skimmed across the grass to snatch it out of the air. Willie's skills had far outgrown his father's teaching. He was ready for bigger challenges now.

Playing with the Gray Sox, Willie earned about a hundred dollars a month, more than twice the amount most of his friends were earning in their part-time jobs. Still, what Willie really wanted was a chance to play in the Negro Leagues, where the best black players competed before big, enthusiastic crowds. By the age of 16, he had become a member of the Black Barons, one of the best teams in the Negro Leagues.

That same year, 1947, Willie watched with keen interest as Jackie Robinson broke the color barrier by joining the formerly all-white Brooklyn Dodgers. At home, though, Willie was busy dealing with his own prejudice problem. The Black Barons had trouble believing that a 16-year-old kid, who was more than 10 years younger than some of his teammates, should be playing with them. Just as Jackie had to prove himself to the white players, Willie had to prove himself to the older players.

Willie answered their doubts by getting two hits in his first game with the Barons. From then on, no one on the team grumbled about him. The young outfielder who was so brilliant on the diamond spent the fall and winter in a classroom finishing his education. His father was determined that Willie would graduate from high school before he began traveling as a professional player.

Willie came to the major leagues as a 20-year-old rookie centerfielder for the National League's New York Giants in 1951. That season another rookie, Mickey Mantle, was playing centerfield for the Yankees. And the Brooklyn Dodgers had their own star centerfielder, Duke Snider. New York fans still argue over who had the greatest centerfielder in the 1950s.

The Giants and the Dodgers finished the season tied for first. They split the first two games of a three-game playoff and then, with the Dodgers ahead 4–2 in the deciding game, Willie stood in the on-deck circle in the bottom of the ninth inning.

Willie's teammate, Bobby Thomson, was at bat against Ralph Branca of the Dodgers. Willie was terrified. He prayed Bobby would do well at the plate because he was afraid that the team and fans would look to him for a hit with the pennant hanging in the balance. Bobby swung and hit a three-run homer, "the shot heard 'round the world," which gave the Giants the pennant. It was the last time Willie Mays hoped to skip the limelight when the game was on the line.

His major league career spanned 22 seasons. Though the Giants moved to San Francisco in 1958, taking Willie with them, he ended his career in New York, playing for the Mets. And despite arguments about the three great New York centerfielders of the 1950s, Willie Mays is considered by many to be baseball's all-time greatest player.

WILLIE MAYS'S CAREER HIGHLIGHTS:

- **Rookie of the Year, 1951.**
- **National League Most Valuable Player, 1954 and 1965.**
- **Lifetime home runs—660 (only Hank Aaron and Babe Ruth hit more).**
- **Won NL home run crown, 1955, 1962, 1964 and 1965.**
- **Gold Glove winner 11 times (1958–1968).**
- **Inducted into the Hall of Fame, 1979.**
- **24 All-Star Game appearances, 1954–1973.**

Babe Ruth.

Superstar shortstop Honus Wagner played for the Pittsburgh Pirates.

NEW YORK — A GREAT STATE FOR BASEBALL

New York State has been home to major league baseball teams since the game began. Did you know that . . .

- New York teams since the 19th century have included the Buffalo Bisons, the Troy Haymakers, the Syracuse Stars, the Brooklyn Bridegrooms, Wonders, Gladiators and Trolley-Dodgers (later, simply the Brooklyn Dodgers), the New York Atlantics, Metropolitans, Highlanders (later, the New York Yankees), Giants and Mets?
- Baseball's Hall of Fame is located in Cooperstown, New York, home of Abner Doubleday who for many years was considered the man who invented the game? The first five players elected to the Hall of Fame in 1936 were Ty Cobb, Walter Johnson, Christy Mathewson, Babe Ruth and Honus Wagner.
- New York City's current National League team, the Mets, was formed because the Brooklyn Dodgers and the New York Giants had gone West, the Dodgers to Los Angeles and the Giants to San Francisco? The Mets 1962 opening day roster even included a former Dodger, Gil Hodges! Hodges later managed the Mets to their 1969 "miracle" World Series win.
- The New York Yankees have retired 12 players' numbers, more than any other major league team?

Many of baseball's early greats were present at the first induction at the National Baseball Hall of Fame in Cooperstown, New York. In the top row, (Left to Right) Honus Wagner, Grover Alexander, Tris Speaker, Nap Lajoie, George Sisler and Walter Johnson. In the bottom row, (Left to Right) Eddie Collins, Babe Ruth, Connie Mack and Cy Young.

THE BLACK PIONEERS

3

By the mid-1940s, it was clear that major league baseball was not filling its rosters with all of the best available talent. Black players had been shunned by organized baseball since the 1880s. Though there was no formal ban on the hiring of a black man, the professional clubs had an unwritten "understanding" that the teams would be composed of white players only.

Through the years, some light-skinned black ballplayers had unsuccessfully tried to break into professional baseball by claiming to be Indian or Cuban. But most top black players competed in the Negro Leagues, which brought together excellent players from around the country.

When World War II ended in 1945, a few major league owners had decided the time had come to break the color barrier in baseball. It was a touchy situation because there were still plenty of people who preferred to exclude blacks from the major leagues forever.

In late 1945 Branch Rickey, president of the Brooklyn Dodgers, signed Negro Leagues star Jackie Robinson to play for his club. This controversial step would eventually bring a flood of new talent to the major leagues including Satchel Page, who was a rookie at 42, and Larry Doby, whose sparkling career was capped off as manager of the Chicago White Sox. Within two years, other black players were invited to join the major leagues. Their talents as ballplayers were more than matched by their courage, as often they had to fight the abuse and insults of prejudice as hard as they had to compete on the field. Together, these trailblazers paved the way for a better kind of baseball.

Jackie Robinson became the first black player in the National League when he joined the Dodgers' top farm team in Montreal, Canada.

RUNNING IN MACK'S SHADOW

There was nothing quite as wonderful as having a big brother like Mack. Nine-year-old Jackie Robinson watched proudly as the neighborhood boys began to choose sides for their afternoon baseball game. He couldn't wait for the game to start. The first boy chosen, of course, was his brother Matthew, who was nicknamed Mack.

Everyone on the block respected Mack. He could throw a baseball with power and accuracy, hit and field and run like a demon. At 14, he was already a star on the high school track team. All the youngsters on Pepper Street in Pasadena, California, would gather at the athletic field of Muir Technical High School to watch Mack's workouts. They cheered him even at practices.

No one cheered louder or more enthusiastically than Mack's baby brother, Jackie. Mack told his kid brother that he was going to be a professional athlete when he grew up. Athletes earned lots of money, Mack told Jackie, sometimes 50 or 60 dollars a week—all for playing games they loved to play anyway! Jackie didn't doubt for a minute that Mack would achieve his goal. He knew that his brother, like all the Robinsons, never gave up.

Jackie's mother, Mallie Robinson, continued to work alone in the fields of a Georgia plantation to earn a living after her husband had left the family. Mallie had three older boys, Edgar, Frank and Mack, and a girl, Willa Mae. Mallie's youngest, Jackie, had been born in 1919.

A few months after her husband left, Mallie and her children moved to Pasadena to start a new life. She worked as a maid to support her family. In a few years, she had saved enough to buy a small house.

Jackie and his brothers and sister grew up knowing that they were expected to contribute to the family income as soon as they could. The older boys shined shoes and sold newspapers. Little Jackie, at the age of five, earned pennies watering flowers every day for his uncle. When he was a bit older, Jackie also shined shoes and sold newspapers. Jackie's favorite job, however, was working as a hot dog vendor at the local ballpark. He learned to spot a customer, slather a hot dog with mustard, pass the hot dog and make change, all without taking his eyes off the game.

Other times, Jackie just tagged along with Mack. In those days, Mack was *the* Robinson to watch on Pepper Street. Though he loved baseball, his real strength was his speed on the track. Jackie loved being with Mack, so he, too, ran track. On this particular day, Jackie watched eagerly as the two Pepper Street baseball teams were chosen. Then Mack called the proceedings to a halt. "Hey! What about Jackie?" he asked.

The other boys groaned. Jackie was younger, smaller and slower than the others. But because Mack was the star of Pepper Street, if he wanted his brother to play ball with him, they had to let Jackie play.

Jackie jumped up, thrilled at his chance. Mack had taught him to hit a baseball but he had always been left out of the neighborhood games. Now he would have his chance to play.

Jackie took whichever position no one else wanted to play. He played in the outfield, shagged fly balls during batting practice and listened carefully when Mack instructed him on the finer points of the game. It didn't matter to him that he wasn't pitching or playing first base. He was happy just to spend time with Mack and play baseball.

The neighborhood games were wonderful training. Because Jackie was competing with players who were bigger and stronger, he had to work harder than he would have against players his own age. The other boys hoped he would quit, but Jackie never did. As long as Mack coached and encouraged him, Jackie stuck it out. He ignored the boys when they made fun of him. He was there to play baseball—and that's exactly what he did.

The year Mack turned 15, his life suddenly changed. A doctor examining him found evidence of a heart problem. He told Mack that it would probably go away but until it did, he was not to play any kind of sports. Mack had to rest as much as possible. He couldn't even participate in high school gym classes.

Mack was stunned. Overnight, it seemed, all his plans for the future had changed. All his dreams had suddenly faded. There was nothing he could do—nothing, that is, he could do for *himself.* Mack decided to concentrate his energy on Jackie.

Jackie was growing rapidly and becoming a much faster runner. Mack told Jackie they would work together to train him as the family athlete. With Mack coaching from the sidelines, Jackie became a fine athlete. It hurt every time he looked at the big brother who had once been so strong, so unbeatable, but Mack refused to allow Jackie to feel sorry for him. He urged Jackie to become the best he could be.

Jackie did. At Muir High he went out for every sport he could—baseball, football, basketball and track. Mack was always there, boosting his confidence and offering advice. Though temporarily out of the limelight, Mack was still very much a part of Jackie's life.

By the time Mack was 20, his doctor was satisfied that he had outgrown the mysterious illness that had troubled his heart. With a clean bill of health, Mack resumed his track career—with vigor.

Jackie was the proudest kid on Pepper Street during the 1936 Berlin Olympics. As he and his gang watched the newsreel from Germany, they saw American runner Jesse Owens streak across the finish line of the 200-meter dash to win the Olympic gold medal. Four yards behind him was 22-year-old Mack Robinson, winning the silver medal. The two black champions proved that German dictator Adolf Hitler's raving about a white "master race" was ridiculous. The Americans had left the German runners in the dust!

By 1946, 27-year-old Jackie was facing his own racial challenge. He had won glory as an amateur athlete at Pasadena Junior College and later at UCLA, and then had chosen professional baseball as his career. In the early 1940s, black ballplayers were not allowed to play on major league teams. The Negro Leagues were the only place for a black player to use his talents. There were some who saw that this segregation of black and white men on the playing field was unfair, and one man finally decided to do something about it.

His name was Branch Rickey and he ran the Brooklyn Dodgers. He was fiery and independent, and he believed that a good player was a good player—black or white. Rickey knew there were many black ballplayers who had major league talent. Rickey wanted to sign a great black ballplayer and tear down the color barrier in organized baseball. The player he chose to shoulder this enormous responsibility was Jackie Robinson.

Rickey made it clear to Jackie exactly what kind of pressure he would be facing. Jackie would have more to worry about than getting a hit off an opposing pitcher or stealing second base successfully. He would face outrage from some fans and plenty of ugly insults. There might be death threats. His own teammates might refuse to play with him.

By contrast, Jackie's behavior would have to be flawless. He had to play superbly on the field and conduct himself with grace and calm off the field. He could not fight back when he was insulted. He could not retaliate in any way, no matter how much it was called for. All he could do to answer his critics was play his heart out, day after day.

To Jackie, it was worth the risk. The chance to play baseball as a Brooklyn Dodger was a dream come true, one he couldn't pass up. He remembered his childhood experience being an unwanted player in those games with the older boys on Pepper Street. He had been shunned by his teammates before and he was ready to deal with it again.

Rickey was not exaggerating about the difficulties ahead. Jackie joined the Dodgers top farm team in Montreal, Canada, where the fans adored him. In some of the other cities in the International League, fans and opposing players heaped abuse on Jackie. But he was also cheered by black people, some who had never seen a professional baseball game before. They came to the park to see the first black man in the 20th century to play professional baseball with whites. At times, Jackie's nerves frayed, but his playing was largely unaffected.

The Montreal Royals opened the 1946 season on April 18 against the Jersey City

Giants. In his second at bat, Jackie smacked a three-run homer. In his next at bat, he bunted safely and treated the spectators to a sampling of his dazzling base running. First, he stole second base. After moving to third on a grounder, Jackie danced off the base and so upset the pitcher that the pitcher balked (he made an illegal hesitation in his delivery) and Jackie was awarded home. For the day, Jackie had four hits and scored four runs. Not a bad start!

Jackie joined the Dodgers in Brooklyn in the spring of 1947. He wore number 42 and started out playing first base, a tough position for him, because he had been playing second base and shortstop for years. At the moment, though, nothing mattered except that Jackie Robinson had arrived.

It didn't take long for opposing players to realize what that meant. Jackie could hit towering home runs or bunt his way on base. What was worse, he terrified opposing pitchers when he danced back and forth on the base paths. He sometimes rattled them so badly they would balk or walk the batters. Jackie stole bases behind their backs or right in front of their faces! He was so fast and so cagey that it was almost impossible to catch him.

Jackie made baseball history as the man who led the way for players of any race or color to make their way in the major leagues. He did it by competing with players who would have preferred to squeeze him out of the game, as the old gang on Pepper Street had once tried to squeeze him out. Jackie, who had watched the

Jackie Robinson was a member of the class of 1935 at Washington Junior High School.

older brother he idolized streak to an Olympic medal, kept running on his own. Jackie wasn't quite as fast as Mack, but his runs touched many people.

JACKIE ROBINSON'S CAREER HIGHLIGHTS:

- First black man in the 20th century to play major league baseball, 1947.
- Rookie of the Year, 1947.
- National League Most Valuable Player, 1949.
- Led the NL in hitting (.342 average), 1949.
- Led the NL in stolen bases, 1947 and 1949.
- Lifetime batting average—.311.
- Inducted into the Hall of Fame, 1962.

When Satchel Paige joined the Cleveland Indians in 1948 at the age of 42, he became the oldest rookie ever.

FROM ROCKS TO RECORDS

Lula Paige always claimed that it was a mistake at the courthouse. She knew perfectly well when her son Leroy was born. When she went to the courthouse in Mobile, Alabama, to report his birth, though, the clerk at the counter wrote down the wrong date. Lula repeated the date and told the clerk he had made a mistake. But the man had no eraser, and claimed he couldn't correct the mistake without one. It was a busy morning, and he told Mrs. Paige he would change the date when he wasn't so busy.

He never did. Whatever the true birth date is, most people believe that Leroy Paige was born on July 7, 1906, in Mobile. He was the seventh child of John and Lula Paige, who eventually had 11 sons and daughters. To support the family, John worked as a gardener and Lula took in washing.

Though they worked hard, the Paiges could never afford toys or games for their children. There was barely enough money for food and the rent on their four-room house on South Franklin Street. So the children played with ordinary objects instead of real toys.

Six-year-old Leroy found that throwing rocks was lots of fun. He was a lanky boy with long arms and legs. Using his right arm and aiming a rock at a rusty can set on a tree stump, he almost always knocked the can down.

As his throwing arm became more powerful, Leroy used it in his household chores. His mother kept chickens at home so that she could fix chicken suppers for the family. One of Leroy's jobs was to kill a chicken for her to cook. His arm had pinpoint accuracy, and Leroy could kill the selected chicken by throwing a rock at its head. It was faster and cleaner than wringing the chicken's neck and it gave Leroy more chances to practice his throwing.

Leroy had other chores as well. When he was very young, his mother sent him out to collect glass bottles which he sold for a few cents each. Soon, though, Lula heard all about a job for Leroy that would bring in better money. Some of the boys in the neighborhood were carrying bags for railroad passengers at the nearby Union

Station. Leroy could earn a nickel or a dime for every bag he carried. At the end of a day, he could bring home a dollar or more for the family.

So seven-year-old Leroy trudged down to Union Station. He quickly found that he could not carry more than two bags at a time. He noticed that the other boys had the same problem. They might spend 15 or 20 minutes carrying one or two bags out of the station, cutting down the amount of money they might be earning.

One day Leroy figured out that he could carry more bags if he used more than just his two arms to carry them. At home, he rigged up a long pole with some thick pieces of rope. The next day, Leroy balanced the pole over his shoulders and under his arms. He tied some bags to his ropes and carried others in his hands. As he walked out of the station, his entire body was hidden under the suitcases.

One of Leroy's friends spotted him as he moved carefully through the station, balancing his burden. "You look like a walking satchel tree!" the friend laughed. A satchel is a traveling bag and, from that time on, Leroy was known as "Satchel" Paige.

At the train station, Satchel was too busy to exercise his throwing arm, but he had lots of chances to throw rocks on his way to school. Unfortunately, he threw for self-defense, not for fun. Satchel and his other black friends attended W.H. Council School a few miles away. On the way to Council, Satchel and his friends had to pass a school for white children.

The white boys often jeered at Satchel and the others. Satchel hated being called ugly names. His powerful, accurate right arm was his best weapon. He fought back by throwing rocks at the white boys who were abusing him and his friends.

Usually, the rocks led to fist fights. Sometimes Satchel and the others had to go to the police station. Satchel felt he had only been defending himself, but Lula was always upset when Satchel got into trouble. To avoid the fights, Satchel often simply didn't go to school.

Life took a turn for the better when Satchel was 10. W.H. Council held baseball tryouts for the boys and coach Wilbur Hines picked Satchel to play first base and the outfield.

In the middle of the season, the team lost two of its pitchers. Hines had watched Satchel throw the ball from the outfield and he could see that he had both power and accuracy in his right arm. Even though Satchel was one of the youngest players, Hines figured it couldn't hurt to let him try to pitch.

Hines was astounded when young Satchel struck out the first three batters he faced. The ball buzzed across the plate so fast the batters could hardly see it. By the end of the game, Satchel had struck out 16 batters and he had not given up a single hit. It was an amazing performance for a 10-year-old who had never pitched a game before!

Immediately, Hines made Satchel the team's number-one pitcher. Satchel's father was very proud of him. He asked whether Satchel would like to be a baseball player when he grew up instead of a gardener. Satchel definitely wanted to be a baseball player. He knew he'd found the great love of his life.

But the Paige family had no money to help Satchel realize his goal. It was frustrating for Satchel not to have a ball or bat to practice with. It was frustrating to

Satchel Paige played for the Kansas City Monarchs in the Negro League.

play baseball only when the W.H. Council team played. He wanted to play all the time!

Satchel wandered into a local toy store one day when he was 12. He looked long and hard at the shelves filled with bright, new, colorful toys—cards and games and sports equipment. He had never owned any store-bought toys. Even though he knew it was wrong, he couldn't resist reaching for a handful of toy rings. In a moment, he had slipped them in his pocket.

As Satchel walked out of the store, trembling, the owner stopped him. In a short while Satchel was down at the police station again. To make matters worse, the police not only discussed the theft of the rings but they also talked to the school's truant officer. It was her job to make sure the children came to school regularly and behaved themselves while they were there.

The truant officer told the police that Satchel often skipped school. The truancy, the fights and now the shoplifting resulted in Satchel being sent to live at the Industrial School for Negro Children at Mt. Meigs, an hour from his home in Mobile.

Like Babe Ruth before him, Satchel found himself surrounded by other boys who were considered problems at home. The staff at Mt. Meigs wanted to help the boys and made an effort to find activities that the boys liked.

During his first week at Mt. Meigs, Satchel tried out for the baseball team. The coach was impressed with his pitching. After practice was over, he said to Satchel, "That arm might do you some good someday. Put all that feeling you put into throwing rocks into throwing baseballs, and you might make something of yourself."

It was good advice. Over the next five and a half years at Mt. Meigs, Satchel grew into a tall, wiry young man who could pitch with amazing speed and accuracy. He often used a windmill windup, where his big size-14 left foot almost came up into his face. He then leaned so far back that his elbows almost touched the ground. When his foot came down, the ball was off and blazing toward the plate.

His accuracy was breathtaking. It was not enough for Satchel to throw the ball over home plate. That was too easy for him. So sometimes he set a chewing-gum wrapper on the plate and then he threw the ball right over the wrapper! None of the players had ever seen anything like it.

In 1923, when Satchel was 17, he was released from Mt. Meigs and sent home. By now his brother Wilson was earning a living as a pitcher and catcher with the Mobile Tigers, an all-black baseball team which had its own field at Eureka Gardens.

One day Satchel was watching the team practice. He saw a boy approach the Tigers manager and ask for a pitching tryout. The manager agreed. The boy took the mound and threw 10 pitches. The manager hit all of them. He told the boy the Tigers didn't need him.

Satchel knew that he could pitch better than that. He asked the manager for a tryout. At first, the manager said no. But because Satchel was the brother of one of his players, he finally agreed to give the youngster a chance.

Satchel took the mound and promptly fired his 10 pitches. The manager not only couldn't hit them, he could hardly *see* them! He gave Satchel a pitching job on the spot.

From that time on, Satchel pitched on black teams all over the country. Conditions were tough for the players on those teams. They were not permitted to stay in many hotels, especially in the South. Often they were not allowed to eat in the town restaurants. They slept on the rickety buses that took them from one game to another, and sometimes they ate breakfasts of hot dogs and warm soda at the ballpark.

Despite Satchel's amazing ability, the major league clubs wanted nothing to do with him. He was still a black man, and at the time only whites were allowed in the majors.

In 1947, Jackie Robinson, who had played with and against Satchel on several black teams, broke into the major leagues as a Brooklyn Dodger. Soon other young black players followed. Satchel was a legendary pitcher but major league teams knew he had developed habits of skipping games or showing up late in the Negro Leagues. They were also afraid that he was simply too old.

They were wrong. Satchel had played for more than 20 years, often pitching every day. His fastball still blazed and his other pitches still kept hitters off balance. Finally, in 1948, Satchel came to the major leagues as a pitcher for the Cleveland Indians. He won six games for the Indians and lost one. He even pitched in that year's World Series! At the end of the season, he was named Rookie of the Year—at the age of 42, he was easily the oldest rookie ever to win the honor.

Satchel later pitched for the St. Louis Browns, and twice he played on American League All-Star teams. In between major league assignments, he often played on black teams.

In 1965, Satchel pitched three innings of scoreless ball for the Kansas City Athletics. He was 59, the oldest player ever to perform in the major leagues!

None of the amazing statistics that Satchel compiled during his many years in the Negro Leagues are recognized by major league baseball. Sadly, the achievements of many great players in the Negro Leagues have gone largely unnoticed and unappreciated. To help correct this situation, the Hall of Fame decided that outstanding players from the Negro Leagues would be admitted to the Hall by a special committee.

In 1971, Satchel was inducted into the Hall of Fame in Cooperstown as the first representative of the Negro Leagues. It was the proudest moment of his life.

SATCHEL PAIGE'S CAREER HIGHLIGHTS:

- **Pitched more than 2,500 games, more than any other pitcher.**
- **Pitched more than 300 shutouts and 55 no-hitters.**
- **Rookie of the Year, 1948.**
- **Selected to the All-Star team, 1952 and 1953.**
- **Inducted into the Hall of Fame, 1971.**

Larry Doby was the first black player in the American League.

A MATTER OF PRIDE

I t isn't every kid who spends his early years in three or four different homes, in different towns, even in different states. Maybe any kid who had would have developed a sense of independence and aloofness that protected himself from feeling like an outsider. Maybe that made it easier for young Lawrence Doby to cope.

The grandson of former slaves, Lawrence Eugene Doby was born on December 13, 1923, in a very poor section of Camden, South Carolina. Camden was a resort town and the site of the annual Carolina Cup horse race. Lawrence's father, David, had worked with racehorses since he was a young boy. His summer job was grooming the horses owned by his wealthy employers in Saratoga, New York, but each winter he returned to Camden.

David's long months away from his wife, Etta, strained their marriage. Finally, Etta decided she didn't want to wait for David to come home anymore so she left young Lawrence with her mother, Augusta Brooks, and went to New Jersey to work as a maid.

Everyone called Lawrence "Bubba," and eventually he took his grandmother's last name. For several years, in fact, he thought his real name was Bubba Brooks, not Lawrence Doby. He considered himself the man of the house and helped his grandmother with her work as a laundress for a local white family. As a young child, Bubba used his little red wagon to pick up and deliver the laundry and haul ice for white families. He also worked in his grandmother's vegetable patch, chopped wood, fed the chickens and sometimes even picked cotton, for which he was paid one dollar for a 12-hour day.

Bubba's heavy responsibilities made him mature beyond his years. He always had a strong sense of his own dignity. Bubba's dignity became a joke among his young friends. When he was five, he and the other boys played down on Market Street, where wealthy white people often tossed coins to the children out of the windows of their horse-drawn carriages. The little boys would scramble for the money, then approach the carriages with their heads bent over. It was a foolish superstition among some white people of the time that rubbing a black child's head was "lucky."

Along with the other boys, Bubba grabbed for the coins that were tossed. But he refused to let a white person rub his head for luck. He had too much pride.

Though Augusta Brooks earned very little money, she managed to keep Bubba fed and clothed. But during the summer of 1934, when Bubba was 10, Augusta began to act strangely. For instance, once she jumped out the window and started running off. Bubba ran after her and brought her home. When Bubba's mother returned home briefly, she saw that Augusta was not well and could no longer take care of her son. Augusta went into a hospital and Bubba went to live with his Aunt Alice and Uncle James Doby.

In Aunt Alice's home, the bewildered boy had not only a new home and family, but also a new—or rather, an *old*—name. Bubba Brooks became Lawrence Doby again overnight. It was the first time he remembered being called by that name and it took him a while to get used to it.

That same summer, Lawrence's father died in New York while on a fishing trip. Lawrence hardly remembered his father. He simply knew that a lot of things seemed to be happening all at once.

For the next four years, Lawrence lived a happy, comfortable family life with his aunt, uncle and five cousins. He attended an excellent black school called the Browning Home-Mather Academy where he had good teachers who cared about him. He played organized sports for the first time and found that he liked them.

Unfortunately, this happy home was not permanent. Lawrence's mother invited him to visit her during the summers of 1937 and 1938 in Paterson, New Jersey, where she worked as a maid. After the second summer she insisted that he remain in Paterson with her. She thought Lawrence would have a better future in the North than in the South.

But moving to New Jersey only made Lawrence feel lonely and out of place. Etta lived in the maid's room in the home of her white employers and there was no room for her son there. Etta arranged for Lawrence to live with a friend of hers who had a house nearby. Etta visited him on her one day off every week.

The sense of security that Lawrence had felt with his Doby relatives in Camden faded living with a stranger in a new town. He saw his mother only once a week, and as a young child he had hardly seen her at all. Augusta Brooks had really been the first parent he had ever known. Now it seemed as though he was starting all over again.

With each move to a new place and a new situation, Lawrence was building a wall of privacy to protect himself. Since he was constantly thrust into different environments, he needed a way to cushion the pain and shock of each change. To the end of his life, he could not throw himself into a friendship right away or trust anyone on first sight. He gave the impression that he preferred to remain distant from everyone.

The boys who got to know Lawrence in Paterson called him Larry and thought he was a little strange. Though all of them were black, Larry carried himself with dignity that was unfamiliar to the others. Of course, Larry's behavior hid his pain

Larry Doby played for the Cleveland Indians from 1948 to 1955.

and loneliness. But to most people it seemed that Larry thought he was something special. He didn't win friends easily.

But Larry had no trouble winning admiration for his athletic talents. At Eastside High School, he was one of only 25 blacks in a student body of 1,200. By the time he graduated in 1942, Larry had earned 11 varsity letters! When he received his last letter at a school assembly, the students gave him a thunderous ovation.

From then on, no one could ignore his excellence in sports, especially in baseball.

Larry began to play professionally in the Negro League in the early 1940s. After a tour of duty in the Pacific during World War II, he returned to baseball.

Shortly after Jackie Robinson became the first black player in the National League, Bill Veeck, the owner of the Cleveland Indians, started looking for a black player from the Negro Leagues to play for him. He settled at last on the Negro National League's leading hitter, Larry Doby. Larry became the American League's first black player.

Larry faced the suspicion and prejudice he encountered in the major leagues with the same reserve he had relied on throughout his life. He had learned early to say as little as possible in any kind of threatening situation. As far as Larry was concerned, it was always best to let his play speak for him.

His play spoke loud and clear. From 1947 through 1959, Larry played sparkling ball, earning seven All-Star Game appearances. In 1954, he led the league in home runs and runs batted in.

After they won the fourth game of the World Series in 1948, Larry and Cleveland teammate Steve Gromek were photographed hugging each other. It was the first time America had seen a picture of a white ballplayer and a black ballplayer embracing in the joy of victory. That picture was worth more than a thousand words for it showed that people of any race, working together, could find joy in their shared achievements.

LARRY DOBY'S CAREER HIGHLIGHTS:

- Seven times named to the All-Star team, 1949–1955.
- Led American League in home runs, 1952 and 1954 (32 each year).
- Had 100-plus RBIs in five different seasons.
- Managed the Chicago White Sox, 1978. (He was the second black man to manage a major league team.)

Kenesaw Mountain Landis.

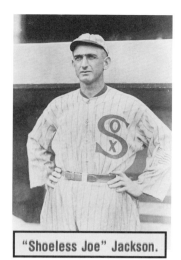

"Shoeless Joe" Jackson.

Ernie Banks.

CHICAGO: A RICH BASEBALL TRADITION

The city of Chicago boasts millions of baseball fans, as well as many years of exciting baseball history. Did you know that . . .

- Some of the Chicago Cubs' fans are called the Bleacher Bums, in honor of the seats where they sit and taunt opposing teams?
- The Chicago Cubs had a longtime superstar, shortstop and first baseman Ernie Banks, who appeared in 14 All-Star Games but never played in a World Series?
- Chicago's Wrigley Field was the last major league ballpark to install lights? Until 1989, every game at Wrigley Field was played during the day!
- Chicago once boasted two all-black clubs? The Chicago Leland Giants were managed from 1906 to 1910 by Andrew "Rube" Foster, a black pitcher whose baseball instincts brought the Leland Giants tremendous recognition and acclaim in Chicago. Then, in 1910, Foster left the Leland Giants to form his own team, the Chicago Union Giants. Along with their regular schedule, the Union Giants played an exhibition game against the 1910 world champion Detroit Tigers, a team which featured Ty Cobb!
- The greatest scandal in baseball history occurred in 1919, when eight team members of Chicago's White Sox were accused of conspiring to fix the outcome of the World Series? These eight men, afterwards called "the Black Sox," were acquitted of criminal charges but were forever barred from professional baseball by the first Commissioner of Baseball, Kenesaw Mountain Landis.

BROTHERS

4

A love and talent for baseball is often passed down from father to son, and from older brother to younger brother. It's not unusual to see more than one star player emerge from a talented family.

What happens when brothers play in the major leagues? It has happened on numerous occasions. Brothers have played on the same team and they've played against each other. Brothers have played every position. On September 15, 1963, the San Francisco Giants had the three Alou brothers—Felipe, Jesus and Matty—in the outfield at the same time. The Delahanty clan, however, holds the record for most brothers to reach the majors with five. Among them, Ed, Frank, Jim, Joe and Tom Delahanty played every position except catcher.

Other brothers have been pitchers. Jim and Gaylord Perry spent most of their careers on different teams, but for a short time during the 1975 season, the Perrys played together for the Cleveland Indians.

Major league baseball's winningest brother combination, Phil and Joe Niekro, pitched on a number of different teams before playing together for the Yankees. By far the most crazy and colorful brothers were Dizzy and Daffy Dean, both pitchers for the St. Louis Cardinals "Gashouse Gang." The double ties of family and baseball have produced some remarkable hotshot brothers, brothers who have competed against one another and have played together as teammates.

Daffy (left) and Dizzy Dean, stars of the 1934 Gashouse Gang.

GASHOUSE SMOKE

The Dean brothers were what you might call "colorful." Colorful and close-knit. Though their personalities were as different as they could possibly be, the brothers always stuck together.

They grew up in Southern farm country. The older brother, Jay Hanna Dean, was born in 1911. When he was asked by reporters where he was born, he always gave different answers. To some he said he was born in Lucas, Arkansas; to others he said Bond, Mississippi; to still others he said Holdenville, Oklahoma. He always said he didn't want reporters to get chewed out by their editors for bringing back the same story someone else had. It was his idea of a great joke. It is generally believed he was born in Arkansas.

The facts aren't clear about Jay's real name, either. Though he was named Jay Hanna by his parents, it seems he took another name in childhood. He had a close friend named Jerome Harris who died at a young age. So Jay Hanna Dean, in tribute to his friend, decided to call himself Jerome Herman Dean.

Jay was interested in everything around him. He was a restless boy, eager to try new things. Sitting still in a classroom was nearly impossible for him. He didn't like to study.

His parents worked hard on the land to earn a living and didn't press him to stay in school. So Jay quit after the fourth grade.

Jay was happy traveling with his family, working wherever they worked instead of going to school. When he was old enough, he became a field worker. He picked cotton for 50 cents a day. When he felt he'd earned enough to get along for a while, he would spend a day playing baseball instead. Jay figured it was silly to waste a nice day working when he could be playing.

Paul Dean was a different breed than his brother Jay. He was born in 1914, two-and-a-half years after Jay, and it quickly became obvious that the two brothers were complete opposites. Where Jay was loud, restless and sometimes lazy, Paul was quiet and far more serious. Like brothers do, though, the boys stuck together and helped each other when they could. And they shared a fondness for baseball.

Paul was only 13 when he had to say good-bye to his older brother. Jay had decided that he hated working in the cotton fields and decided that joining the

Jay (Dizzy) Dean's stunning pitching and zany antics attracted crowds to the ballpark.

Army was the fastest way out of the fields. So he signed up in 1927, at the age of 16.

When Jay got out of the Army, he returned to an earlier interest—baseball.

While he was pitching in a Texas sandlot game, Jay caught the eye of a scout from the St. Louis Cardinals. He signed with the Cardinals in the fall of 1929 and the following year he rushed through the Cardinals farm system and was sent to St. Louis, where he got his first major league start in the final game of the season. He allowed only three hits and one run and earned a victory.

Though he was to spend one more season pitching in the minors, on the basis of that one game the brash young pitcher demanded to see Branch Rickey, then the team general manager. Dean insisted he was worth more than a salary of $3,000 for the following season. Rickey was dazed by the boy's incredible demands. Dean had, after all, only pitched one major league game in his life!

Rickey discovered that arguing with Jay Dean was too much trouble, and he eventually agreed to pay him more money. Jay promised to bring more people to the ballpark—and with his stunning pitching and zany antics he did just that.

Paul (Daffy) Dean won two World Series games as a rookie pitcher for the Cardinals.

Meanwhile, Paul was growing up. Just as his brother had done, he took to base-ball right away. As a kid, he had pitched with Jay, and learned his brother's tricks. Now he was learning some of his own. Like Jay, Paul threw a smoking fastball to get hitters out.

Jay became known as "Dizzy" Dean for his wacky and outgoing personality as well as for the dizzy state he left opposing batters in. In 1932, Dizzy became a permanent part of the pitching rotation for St. Louis. The club was becoming known as "The Gashouse Gang," a fiery, riotous group of players who didn't shave before games, wore dirty uniforms and put on the best show in baseball. The center of it all, of course, was Dizzy Dean. He loved entertaining the fans and outraging the Cardinals management. No one was ever sure which activity he enjoyed more.

The fun increased in 1934 when Dizzy's brother Paul joined the Cardinals as a 20-year-old rookie with a blazing fastball. Though his personality was completely different than Dizzy's, Paul was dubbed "Daffy" by the press, which found the com-bination of brothers named Dizzy and Daffy irresistible. His teammates always called him Paul.

As a pitching duo, the brothers dazzled the baseball world. Dizzy was an established Cardinals star, and with the season still young, the rookie Paul had already won five games. It looked as though he might turn out to be as valuable as his brother.

Dizzy wasn't happy. He thought Branch Rickey was not only underpaying him, but that he was also underpaying Paul. Dizzy insisted early in 1934 that Paul be given a $2,000 raise. When Rickey indignantly refused, the Dean brothers went on strike. They refused to get into uniform, much less pitch, until Dizzy's demands were met. Rickey would not relent and the brothers soon grew worried over how well the team was faring without them. It wasn't long before the Deans were back in uniform.

By now, it was clear that the Deans were not always easy to work with. Dizzy refused to take pitching direction from the Cards manager and second baseman, Frank Frisch. Before a crucial doubleheader late in the 1934 season, Frisch tried to advise Dizzy on how to pitch to each of the Brooklyn Dodgers. Dizzy finally told him, "It don't look exactly right for an infielder like you to be tellin' a star like me how I should pitch."

Frisch was outraged. He told Dizzy that if he didn't pitch the way he was told, the Dodgers would destroy him. Dizzy cheerfully ignored the instructions. That afternoon, pitching the way he wanted, Dizzy allowed only three hits and won easily.

The second game of the doubleheader was even more dazzling. Paul pitched for St. Louis and his fastball was knocking out batters as fast as they came up; he ended up pitching a no-hitter! Afterward, his older brother strolled over to him. "Hey, Paul," Dizzy greeted him. "If you'd-a told me you was goin' to pitch a no-hitter, why, I'd-a-pitched one, too!"

The St. Louis Cardinals were the National League champions in 1934. In the World Series, they met the Detroit Tigers, who featured the great slugger Hank Greenberg.

Dizzy had begged Frank Frisch for the chance to pitch four games in a row. After the hard labor of his cotton-picking days and his later years in the sandlots, Dizzy thought nothing of pitching four tough games, one each day. Frisch refused, telling him it was impossible. Dizzy did end up starting three games in the series. Paul pitched twice.

In the last game, Frisch yelled at Dizzy as Hank Greenberg came up, "Don't give him anything chest high!" Dizzy promptly threw a letter-high fastball. Greenberg lashed the ball into centerfield. Frisch groaned.

"Hey, Frank," Dizzy called back admiringly. "You was right!"

The Gashouse Gang won the Series. Not surprisingly, the Dean brothers had pitched all four winning games! They had also racked up an amazing number of regular-season wins. Dizzy had won 30 games and Paul 19!

Dizzy's career suffered a big blow at the 1937 All Star Game, where he was hit on the foot by a line drive that broke his big toe. With his foot aching, Dizzy couldn't throw with his usual motion. He changed his pitching motion to ease the pain in his foot. As a result, he hurt his arm and never pitched as well again.

Paul Dean's career was always linked to his brother's. Some say that Paul was a fine pitcher whose reputation suffered from his being so closely associated with

Dizzy. He was always overshadowed by his one-of-a-kind brother. The Dean brothers are a special part of any recollection of the 1934 Gashouse Gang. They may have been Dizzy and Daffy, but they were also dazzling.

DIZZY DEAN'S CAREER HIGHLIGHTS:

- **Last pitcher in National League to win 30 games in a single season, 1934.**
- **Led the NL in strikeouts four straight years, 1932–1935.**
- **Led the NL in complete games, four straight years, 1933–1936.**
- **Elected to the Hall of Fame, 1953.**

DAFFY DEAN'S CAREER HIGHLIGHTS

- **Won two World Series games as a rookie pitcher, 1934.**

While brothers Joe (standing) and Phil Niekro are both pitchers, they differ in everything from personalities to pitching styles.

PHIL AND JOE NIEKRO

BOUND BY A PITCH

The Niekros were a close-knit family. Like all close-knit families, they had something important binding them together. For some families, it is religion or politics or careers. For the Niekros, it was the knuckleball.

Phil Niekro, Sr. had been a fine amateur pitcher during his younger years in the 1920s. Like many other boys, he had dreamed of a career in the major leagues. One Sunday afternoon, the dream slipped away from him. He started to pitch a game without warming up his arm. Within a few minutes, the strain of throwing hard with a cold arm tore the muscles in his arm. He was never able to pitch the same way again.

After his pitching injury, Phil, Sr. developed a special pitch called a knuckleball. It was a pitch that didn't spin on its way to the plate, but instead fluttered unpredictably like a butterfly. Most hitters couldn't figure out where it was going, let alone how to hit it! Phil, Sr. thought it was great.

He and his wife, Ivy, settled into a small home in Lansing, Ohio, a tiny town 70 miles south of Pittsburgh, Pennsylvania. Lansing depended completely on the nearby coal mines for its livelihood and, like so many others, Phil worked in the mines. In his spare time, he practiced the knuckleball. He wanted to perfect it and pass it on to his children.

The Niekros' first child was not a son as Phil had hoped, but that didn't stop Phil. Not long after his daughter Phyllis began to toddle, Phil taught her to throw the tricky pitch.

Mrs. Niekro gave birth to a son, Phil, Jr. in 1939. When Phil, Sr. began to teach his son about his favorite game, Phyllis became the family's designated catcher.

Phil, Jr. took to the special pitch just as his father had. By the time he was seven, little Phil was throwing knuckleballs to his sister while his father watched proudly. Five years after Phil, Jr. was born, another boy, Joe, joined the family.

It was obvious that the two brothers shared their dad's passion for baseball but they played the game in different ways. Phil had big hands that were ideal for throwing his father's special pitch. Joe's fingers were too small to throw the

69

knuckleball, but his fastball burst across the plate.

The boys' personalities differed in the same way their favorite pitches did. Phil, Jr. had his knuckleball, a quirky, funny pitch that always got attention. Phil himself was colorful, enthusiastic, and always interested in being part of whatever went on in the community. Joe had his fastball, which was basic and dependable. Joe was quieter and less flashy than his brother. Yet the two got along just fine.

And they shared some unusual training! Lansing, like much of Ohio, was home to many Polish families. Polka music was very popular with these families, and the Niekro boys learned to dance the polka. Their mother thought it was important to teach them something besides sports. Phil, Sr. just figured that dancing the polka was a good way to strengthen their legs for baseball.

Both Phil and Joe were awed by their friend John Havlicek, who played every sport brilliantly but was especially magical on the basketball court. There didn't seem to be anything he couldn't do with a basketball in his hands.

John taught the Niekro brothers to train seriously for a sport. He rose every morning at six so that he could practice on the school playground before class. He also kept Phil and Joe company while they pedaled their bicycles on the streets. John didn't own a bike, so he ran or jogged beside them. He was so motivated that he often ran faster than they could pedal.

Phil Niekro's specialty was the knuckleball his father taught him.

John drew most of the attention from scouts when he and Phil, Jr. were in high school. Phil knew that despite his knuckleball, he didn't yet have enough to offer major league ball clubs. Good pitching prospects had fastballs that blazed by hitters at 90 miles an hour. Phil's best fastball was about 65 miles an hour. It wasn't likely to impress many baseball scouts.

Fortunately, Phil didn't have to compete with John Havlicek for the attention of baseball scouts. John had already settled on a basketball career. Eventually, he became a superstar with the Boston Celtics.

Phil also wasn't competing with his brother Joe. With more than five years between them, Joe would not be ready for the major leagues for some time. In fact, Phil wondered whether they would ever have the chance to play together. After all, by the time Joe came up, Phil might already have retired! But as it turned out, like the Dean brothers, not only did the Neikros play in the same league, they ended up on the same team.

As they grew older, their personalities and careers became more alike. Phil worked harder on his fastball, to balance the wild knuckleball that carried his career from team to team. He pitched for 20 years in Milwaukee and Atlanta for the Braves. He finished his career with the New York Yankees and the Cleveland Indians. Joe finally developed a pitch to go with his exploding fastball. Naturally, it was a knuckleball. With the knuckleball in his bag of pitching tricks, he moved from Chicago to San Diego to Atlanta, before an 11-year stop in Houston. Then it was on to New York and Minnesota. The brothers were together with the Yankees at the end of the 1985 season.

Phil was 46 years old. His knuckleball placed less stress on his arm than the fastball favored by most pitchers. Hard-throwing pitchers often had to end their careers early. Because Phil relied mostly on that funny butterfly pitch and because he threw it easily, his career had already lasted more than twenty years.

On October 6, 1985, Phil, Sr. was in the hospital in Wheeling, West Virginia. He had recently had stomach surgery and lay in the hospital's intensive care unit. Patients in intensive care are critically ill and any drop in their condition is very serious.

That night, Phil was facing a milestone in his baseball career: He had an opportunity to win his 300th ball game. Few pitchers last long enough in the majors to win 300 ball games. Only 17 pitchers had done it in the history of the game at that time.

Phil was to pitch in Toronto, Canada against the Blue Jays. He wasn't sure he wanted to pitch because he felt he should be with his father at the hospital. But Phil was already 46 and he might not get another chance for 300.

When Phil, Jr. visited his father in the hospital, Phil, Sr. had rallied enough to write his son a message. The handwriting was shaky, but the message was clear: *WIN— I'LL BE HAPPY.* When Phil, Jr. began the game against Toronto, the note from his dad was tucked into a pocket of his uniform.

Joe watched as his brother tried for his 300th win. Phil was older than his teammates and was likely to tire more quickly than younger pitchers, especially since it was the end of the season. Joe, a starting pitcher for the Yankees, was ready to relieve his brother if Phil couldn't go the distance. If Phil's 300th victory hung in the balance, Joe wanted to step in to save the game.

As Joe watched Phil pitching to the Toronto batters, he noticed something peculiar. Phil wasn't throwing the knuckleball; he was throwing his fastball. As the game went on, Joe realized that not one pitch had been Phil's famous knuckleball. The pitch Phil, Sr. had taught him, the pitch Phil had relied on throughout his career, was absent on his milestone night.

Joe couldn't figure it out. After four innings, he asked Phil, "When are you gonna throw it?"

Phil laughed. He had already decided he would not throw the knuckleball that night. He was tired of being called "the knuckleball pitcher." He wanted to prove that he could win without it.

By the ninth inning, Phil was still on the mound. The Yankees were ahead, 8-0. Three more outs and he would have his 300th win. And he still had not thrown a single knuckleball.

Phil told Joe that he wanted the shutout as well as the win. "If I lose the shutout," he said, "I'm out of the game. I want you to finish for me."

Joe had seen how well his brother was pitching that night. "Forget it," he told Phil. "Don't even think about it."

Just before the last inning began, Joe came out of the dugout to catch Phil's eight warmup pitches. Phil, always joking, threw him a knuckleball and Joe had to dive out of the way. He hadn't been expecting it!

Phil quickly got the first two outs. He was still throwing only fastballs. Then the Blue Jays Tony Fernandez hit a double to leftfield and Phil began to tense up. Jeff

Burroughs stepped to the plate. Phil threw a fastball, but the life had gone out of it. Burroughs hit it foul for the first strike. The next pitch was a ball. Phil thought for a moment. It was the biggest game of his career. It might even be the last. Why was he holding back the pitch his father had taught him? What better time or place to use it?

Phil threw a knuckleball and Burroughs swung and missed. Phil felt better now. He threw another knuckleball. Burroughs swung and missed again.

Phil had his 300th win. Joe had even better news for him as he came to the dug-out. Phil, Sr. was going to be fine. And it had been his pitch which had won this game—and 299 before it—for his oldest son.

Together, the Niekro brothers won more major league games, 538, than any brother combination.

PHIL NIEKRO'S CAREER HIGHLIGHTS:

- **Lifetime victories, 318.**
- **Three-time 20-game winner, 1969, 1974 and 1979.**

JOE NIEKRO'S CAREER HIGHLIGHTS:

- **Two-time 20-game winner for the Houston Astros, 1979 and 1980.**

Ken Griffey, Sr.

Ken Griffey, Jr.

Mel Stottlemyre.

Todd Stottlemyre.

Bobby Bonds.

Barry Bonds.

FATHERS AND SONS:
FUN FACTS
ABOUT PLAYERS AND
THEIR DADS

Baseball is a game often shared by fathers with their sons. In some cases, the fathers are baseball professionals. In others, the sons use their fathers' advice to become the superstars their fathers never were. Did you know that . . .

- Superstar outfielder Bobby Bonds taught his son Barry the game so well that Barry is now a rising star with the Pittsburgh Pirates?
- Yogi Berra managed his son Dale on the Yankees ball club?
- Former Yankee Mel Stottlemyre's son Todd is a chip off the old block? Todd has pitched for the Toronto Blue Jays since 1988.
- Superstar Orlando Cepeda was not only a great ballplayer in his own right, but is also the son of Perucho Cepeda, one of Puerto Rico's most popular and talented baseball stars?
- Cleveland Indians first baseman Keith Hernandez learned the game from his father John? John was once a promising player whose career ended in the minor leagues when he was hit by a pitched ball. With years of instruction from John, Keith has won 11 Gold Gloves for outstanding work at first base.
- Ken Griffey, Sr. and Ken Griffey, Jr. have played in the major leagues at the same time, Ken, Sr. for the Cincinnati Reds and Ken, Jr. for the Seattle Mariners? Both are outfielders.

STARS OF THE '60s AND '70s

5

By the 1960s, America was changing rapidly. The peace and order of the 1950s had given way to uncertainty, unrest and a very unpopular war in Vietnam. At the same time, many Americans were working hard for civil rights, women's rights and ecology.

Baseball was changing, too. The 1960s and 1970s were notable for many long-standing records being broken. The most remarkable of these was Babe Ruth's lifetime record of 714 home runs, which many people had thought would never be broken. They were wrong. In 1974, Hank Aaron of the Atlanta Braves broke the Babe's record in a game against the Los Angeles Dodgers.

Strikeout records came down when Tom Seaver and Nolan Ryan took the mound. Speed demons such as Lou Brock broke records for stealing bases. And slugger Reggie Jackson jazzed up the diamond as "Mr. October," famous for his extraordinary post-season play.

Due to injuries, Sandy Koufax's pitching career was short, but it included four no-hitters and one perfect game. Tom Seaver's only perfect game came during Little League, although his pursuit of perfection in the major leagues began when he was named Rookie of the Year in 1967 and included three Cy Young awards over a six-year period. In the '60's, Pittsburgh Pirate Roberto Clemente was one of the sport's best with 3,000 career hits. Due to these extraordinary players, the old game would never be the same!

Sandy Koufax pitched four no-hitters in his career, including one perfect game.

YOU HAVE TO BE READY

To New York kids, Coney Island means fun. Located at the southernmost tip of Brooklyn, the famous Coney Island amusement park sits right on the beach. To most people, Coney Island means afternoons of thrill rides and hot dogs and sunburns. To Brooklyn boys in the 1940s, it was also the name of their sandlot baseball league.

One spring, a Brooklyn man named Milt Laurie was managing a Coney Island team called the Parkviews. His players ranged in age from 14 to 17. Laurie sat on the bench next to the field, watching the boys tossing a baseball around the infield. A tall, lanky, dark-haired 17-year-old boy caught his eye.

Unlike the other boys, who seemed to be running or catching or somehow always in motion, this one just stood at first base. Yet when it was his turn to throw the ball to the second baseman, the ball seemed to explode out of his hand.

This kid, Sandy Koufax, didn't really seem interested in playing sandlot baseball. He had only come down to tryouts because his friends wanted to play.

Laurie got up slowly and walked out to first base. "Hey, Koufax. How come you're here at first?"

Sandy looked at the manager. The question didn't make much sense to him. He always played first base at Lafayette High School. Maybe he wasn't much of a first baseman, but then, baseball wasn't really his game. His real love was basketball.

Laurie told Sandy that he was wasting his time at first base. He had a strong arm. Why not try pitching?

Sandy had never thought about pitching before. But Laurie encouraged him and coached him. Sandy's pitches were astonishingly fast. He didn't have much more than a fastball, but it was enough for the Coney Island League. By the end of the season, the Parkviews had won the league title, thanks to Sandy's blazing fastball.

As the schedule wound down, the Parkviews often noticed baseball scouts in the rickety stands next to their field. The scouts were watching Sandy. Other pitchers, knowing they were there, might have gotten rattled. But Sandy couldn't have cared less about baseball scouts. He had already decided what he wanted to do with his life.

So when a few of the scouts talked to him about signing a contract to play professional baseball, Sandy thanked them and politely said no. He didn't want to play baseball, he told them. He was really a basketball player at heart.

Despite Milt Laurie's shrewd appraisal of Sandy's pitching talent, Sandy didn't yet recognize that pitching could be his meal ticket. He simply wasn't ready to commit himself to baseball.

Sanford Koufax was born in Brooklyn, New York, on December 30, 1935. Other Brooklyn boys loved baseball from infancy and rooted hard for Brooklyn's major league team, the Dodgers. Sandy, however, wasn't attracted to baseball. For one thing, it was hard to play a good baseball game on the hard pavement of the Brooklyn streets. The paved streets and sidewalks were far better suited to basketball, so Sandy and his pals played basketball most of the time. It was the perfect game for Sandy. As a nine-year-old, he was already tall, with long arms and legs that were perfect for swishing a basketball through a hoop and pounding up and down a basketball court. By the age of 11, he had joined the team at the local Jewish Community House as a forward.

For Sandy, baseball was an afterthought. Sure, he played with his friends when they couldn't get up a basketball game in the neighborhood. But his two real goals were to keep on playing basketball and to become an architect.

Both goals became possibilities during Sandy's outstanding final basketball season at Lafayette High. College scouts watched the young forward and saw potential. Sandy was just as interested in a college education as he was in basketball. He finally accepted a basketball scholarship from the University of Cincinnati, where he could study architecture as well as play hoops. It seemed perfect.

At 17, in the fall of 1953, Sandy went off to the University of Cincinnati. He played on Cincinnati's basketball team and averaged 10 points a game as a forward.

By the spring, Sandy was antsy. The basketball season was over until the following fall. He half-heartedly tried out for Cincinnati's freshman baseball team. Sandy surprised himself when, in 32 innings, he struck out 51 batters.

The scouts started coming around again and baseball started to catch his interest.

He still wasn't ready for the pros. His fastball was fast all right, but it was often wild. When the New York Giants invited him to a tryout at their stadium, the Polo Grounds, his pitches were as fast as advertised. But when the Giants saw Sandy throwing those pitches all over the stadium, they decided not to pursue him.

The following year, something clicked. Three major league clubs were interested in Sandy. The Milwaukee Braves, the Pittsburgh Pirates and the Brooklyn Dodgers all wanted to sign him. But Al Campanis of the Dodgers wooed Sandy most persuasively.

Campanis met with Sandy and his parents at their home in Brooklyn. He reminded them that Sandy had been born and bred in Brooklyn. A Brooklyn boy should play for a Brooklyn club, he told them. The $14,000 bonus the club offered helped the Koufaxes make up their minds, and Sandy signed with the Dodgers.

Because the Dodgers had given the young pitcher such a large bonus they had to keep him on the roster in Brooklyn. In 1955, 19-year-old Sandy was not yet ready to play at the major league level. In spring training at Vero Beach, Florida, he was so tense and scared that he threw too hard and wound up with a sore arm.

**A young Sanford Koufax
swings the bat.**

When his arm was well again, Sandy went to work pitching batting practice, but most of his pitches were wild and batters spun away from the plate to avoid being hit. Sandy was so embarrassed that the Dodgers pitching coach began to warm him up alone. This saved Sandy the agony of pitching badly in front of his new teammates.

For six years Sandy struggled to put together the kind of season the Dodgers expected of him. Sometimes he would pitch well and get a lot of strikeouts. The Dodgers would be relieved and hopeful. In the next game he would be back to throwing wild pitches, unable to get anyone out. It seemed hopeless.

Finally, in the spring of 1961, something clicked again. One day, Sandy was riding on the Dodgers team bus. His roommate, Norm Sherry, a reserve catcher for the Dodgers, sat down next to him. The pitching coaches, the manager, the front office people had all tried to tell Sandy what was wrong with his pitching. Sandy had listened and tried to correct his mistakes. Somehow, no matter how he tried, the answer seemed to be just beyond him.

On this day, however, Sherry had some advice. "I think you'd have less trouble if you'd just throw easier, Sandy. Take something off your fastball, throw more changeups [change-of-pace pitches]. Just try to get the ball over."

Everyone had said, in one way or another, the same thing to Sandy. This time, though, the words finally meant something. This time Sandy was ready to hear them.

The following day Sandy pitched in an exhibition game between the Dodgers "B" squad and the Chicago White Sox "B" squad. Remembering Sherry's advice, he kept his motion easy. He didn't work as hard to throw the ball over the plate. After loading the bases with a series of wild pitches, the relaxed motion made all the difference. Sandy set down the next three White Sox hitters. No one scored a run. He was finally ready to live up to his potential.

After that important spring of 1961, Sandy Koufax became one of baseball's greatest pitchers ever. He threw four no-hit games, including a perfect game against the Chicago Cubs in September of 1965. In that magic year of 1965, he set a National League strikeout record with 382 and won the second of three Cy Young Awards as the league's top pitcher.

Sandy spent most of the mid 1960s playing in pain. He suffered painful injuries in the forefinger and elbow of his pitching arm. Finally, he developed arthritis, a very painful disease of the joints, in his left arm. At the end of the 1966 season, Sandy decided not to risk further damage to his arm and he announced his retirement from baseball.

Sandy Koufax had a short baseball career but he will always be remembered as one of the game's greatest pitchers.

SANDY KOUFAX'S CAREER HIGHLIGHTS:

- **Lifetime victories—165.**
- **Pitched four no-hitters, including one perfect game.**
- **National League Cy Young Award winner, 1963, 1965 and 1966.**
- **NL Most Valuable Player, 1963.**
- **NL ERA leader for five straight years, 1962–1966.**
- **NL strikeout leader, 1961, 1963, 1965 and 1966.**
- **Inducted into the Hall of Fame, 1972.**

ROBERTO CLEMENTE

A HELPING HAND

The children in the classroom at San Anton in Carolina, Puerto Rico, listened on that day in 1950 as their teacher explained to them that the schoolyard was too overgrown and messy for them to play in safely.

The children, of course, wanted to play anyway. If there was nowhere else to play, they were willing to roll around in the dirt and the weeds. The teacher explained that the school wouldn't allow that. The yard had to be cleaned and unfortunately, hiring people to clean it out would cost the school more money than it could afford.

One of the boys in the back of the room suddenly stood up. He was 15-year-old Roberto Clemente, usually shy and quiet in class. Now his voice rang out as he told the teacher, "It won't cost anything! We've all got strong hands and arms, and everyone is going to pitch in."

To the teacher's surprise, Roberto proved as good as his word. He was an enthusiastic leader and he was good at coaxing the others into working with him on any kind of project. He persuaded the other children to bring hoes from home, and they worked before and after school cleaning up the yard. In a short time, the students had a clean, safe playground, thanks largely to Roberto and his refusal to give up on something that would benefit others.

Roberto Clemente was the youngest of five children born to Melchor and Luisa Clemente of Barrio (the Spanish word for neighborhood) San Anton in Carolina, Puerto Rico. Luisa had two other children from a previous marriage, making Roberto her seventh child when he arrived on August 18, 1934. By the time Roberto was born, his father had risen from laboring in the sugar cane fields to foreman of the Victoria Sugar Mill in Carolina. Roberto lived with his family in a comfortable home with five bedrooms and an indoor bathroom, a luxury at the time. Though Roberto grew up during the tail end of the Depression, when millions of people were out of work and hungry, he and his family always had enough to eat.

Roberto adored his father. Melchor was 53 when his last son was born. Though he was a strict father, he was always affectionate with his children. Melchor became

Roberto Clemente started in the Puerto Rican League playing for the Cangrejeros.

ill when Roberto was about eight years old and had to spend several days in the nearby Presbyterian Hospital. Roberto was too young to visit his father in the hospital, but that didn't stop him checking in on his dad. Every day he climbed a palm tree outside his father's window so he could look in and make sure Melchor was getting better.

From the very beginning, the Clementes' youngest son commanded attention. Although he was shy with adults or children he didn't know, he loved being the leader among his friends.

From the age of five, whenever he earned money for doing chores, he spent it at a coin-operated photo machine that would take your picture when you pushed a button. Roberto loved posing for pictures. His older brothers teased him, saying he must think he was really handsome to be spending his money on photographs of himself. Roberto didn't care. He just loved smiling at the camera and getting the picture out of the little slot. Years later, as an adult, he was never too busy to pose for a picture at the ballpark.

Of course, Roberto had other interests as well. His mother Luisa went to church regularly and took Roberto with her. Roberto loved singing hymns and sometimes he played his favorite, "Only God Makes a Man Happy," on the organ at home.

Roberto's athletic skills also began to develop when he was a child. He had huge hands, which easily grasped the big ball of rags that he and his friends used as a baseball in their games. Soon he began to play baseball with his three older brothers, who were superb players. They taught little Roberto all they knew about the game.

Roberto loved baseball, but he didn't limit himself to one sport. The weather in Puerto Rico is warm for most of the year, which makes it an ideal place to spend a lot of time outdoors. So Roberto competed in track and field along with baseball. By the time he reached high school, he threw the javelin, ran the 400-meter dash and high-jumped. There was even talk that the youngest Clemente might qualify to represent Puerto Rico in the 1956 Olympics!

Still, baseball remained Roberto's great love. Sometimes Melchor would give Roberto bus fare to San Juan, where he went to buy lottery tickets for the family. At the time, Roberto's favorite ballplayer, New York Giants star Monte Irvin, was playing Winter League ball at the Sixto Escobar Stadium a mile from San Juan. Roberto always got off the bus at Sixto Escobar to see part of the game, then walked into San Juan to buy the lottery tickets.

When he was 16, Roberto was playing softball with the Sello Rojo Rice team. It was a team of Carolina players managed by a man named Roberto Marin. The boy from San Anton played shortstop. His arm was so accurate and so powerful that he could cut down almost any runner at the plate. He was also speedy on the base paths and was an excellent hitter.

Roberto Marin believed in the young Clemente. He thought he was an unpolished gem who should be seen by important men in baseball. Marin's friend Pedro Zorrilla owned one of the teams in the Winter League and was also a scout for the Brooklyn Dodgers. When Zorilla saw what Roberto could do, the man offered him a bonus of $5,000 and $60 per month to play baseball for him. Roberto's teammates would include some of America's biggest major league stars who spent their winters in Puerto Rico earning extra money in the Winter League.

The Winter League experience honed Roberto's talent. Many of his teammates, including Willie Mays, spent time coaching him and helping him improve his skills. Eighteen-year-old Roberto was suddenly a ballplayer to watch.

In 1954, the Dodgers held a clinic for 100 or so players at Sixto Escobar Stadium, where Roberto had once watched Monte Irvin play. Now Roberto himself was firing balls from centerfield to home plate. When he ran the 60-yard dash in 6.4 seconds, the scouts were astounded. They asked him to repeat the dash. Again, he ran it in 6.4 seconds. In the batting cage, he hit everything they threw to him.

When he was 19, he was ready to accept the Dodgers' offer to play with their top Montreal farm team—the same team with which Jackie Robinson had debuted eight years before.

The Dodgers didn't hold him for long. In 1955, Roberto was snatched up by the Pittsburgh Pirates. For the rest of his life, he wore a Pirates uniform.

Roberto became a star in Pittsburgh. His fierce desire to win, his hustle and his amazing baseball talent were quickly apparent to everyone. He was a complete ballplayer. He played every game to win, even when he was hurt.

Every winter Roberto returned to Puerto Rico, where he had established a home with his wife, Vera, and their children. As he had in his childhood, Roberto delighted in working on community projects. He maintained a keen interest in his native island. In fact, he was mentioned as a possible candidate for mayor. Though he believed he could do some good for Puerto Rico, he refused to consider the idea because he was afraid people would vote for him just because he was a famous ballplayer.

But Roberto did not refuse to help an earthquake relief expedition in late 1972. A few months before, in September, he had tagged his 3,000th major league hit, a milestone few players have ever reached. Now he planned to go to Nicaragua, where a recent earthquake had devastated the country. Survivors needed food and clothing desperately, and Roberto had spent the last weeks of 1972 collecting supplies for the earthquake victims. To be sure they received the packages quickly, he intended to fly there himself and supervise the distribution.

On New Year's Eve, Roberto's plane took off from San Juan. A few minutes later, fire broke out in the engines. The plane crashed in the Atlantic Ocean and everyone aboard was killed. At the age of 38, Roberto Clemente was dead.

From the beginning of his life to the end, he was a man who always reached out with a helping hand to someone in need. After all, he reasoned, that was what neighbors were for.

Roberto Clemente played for the Pittsburgh Pirates from 1955 until his death in 1972.

ROBERTO CLEMENTE'S CAREER HIGHLIGHTS:

- Career hits—3,000.
- Lifetime batting average—.317.
- National League batting leader, 1961, 1964, 1965 and 1967.
- Gold Glove winner a record 12 times (1961–1972).
- Selected to the All-Star team, 1960–1967 and 1969–1971.
- Elected to the Hall of Fame, 1973.

Pitcher Tom Seaver won 311 major league games.

TOM SEAVER

STRIVING FOR PERFECTION

It was a sunny Saturday in July of 1954 in the central California city of Fresno. The boys of the North Fresno Rotary Little League team spilled onto the baseball diamond at the local junior high school. Their parents and friends were there to cheer them on.

The boys shouted encouragement to each other as they warmed up. They all hollered to their pitcher, number 13, a brown-haired, hazel-eyed nine-year-old who carefully concentrated on the catcher behind home plate. The pitcher's name was George Thomas Seaver, but everyone called him Tom.

The umpire signaled the start of the game. The heat had already risen to over 100 degrees. Everyone was sweating, but Tom didn't even notice the sticky air. His mind was focused completely on the batters.

Five innings passed. Coach Hal Bicknell couldn't believe what he was seeing. His pitcher had not surrendered a single hit to the other side. Not one batter had walked or even reached first base on an error. At the age of nine, Tom Seaver was pitching a perfect game! It was a pitcher's greatest possible achievement.

The sixth and last inning arrived. Tom knew that he was three outs away from a perfect game, a rare achievement for a pitcher at any level. His parents would be so proud!

Charles and Betty Seaver sat in the centerfield stands with Tom's dog, Little Bit, cheering with the others as their son set down the first two batters of the inning. Only one more to go for a perfect game!

Tom's hands began to shake. He wanted this out so badly. His father had taught him to try his hardest in everything he did. Tom threw the first pitch. The umpire called it a ball.

Tom was nervous now. He wanted the game to be over. He threw another pitch, but his control was shaky. The batter realized how excited Tom was. He refused to swing, hoping Tom would walk him.

With the count at two balls and two strikes, Tom threw a perfect strike. The umpire called it a ball and Tom began to shake again.

Calm down, he told himself. *Stay in control.* He took a deep breath and wound up. The ball sailed to the plate. The batter never moved.

"Strike three!" called the umpire. "That's the game!"

The Seavers tumbled out of the stands cheering and laughing, and sprinted onto the field to hug their youngest son. Tom had pitched a perfect game!

Tom learned early how important it was to strive for perfection. His father was an excellent amateur golfer who had victoriously represented America in the Walker Cup competition in 1932. Charles concentrated on his game and never stopped trying to improve himself. Tom was always awed by his father's dedication and hard work.

The Seavers were a family of athletes. Tom's mother, Betty, also played golf. His older brother, Charlie, showed early promise as a football player and his two sisters, Katie and Carol, were swimmers and surfers.

Tom was born on November 17, 1944. By the time he came along, his family was already settled comfortably into a rambling house in Fresno, where his father worked as an executive for a trucking company.

It was a happy, sheltered life. It was also a life of intense competition, especially for little Tom. Being the youngest and smallest in the family, he felt he had to strive harder to keep up with his brother and sisters. From the time he could toddle, his favorite sport was baseball. He was always ready to play, even when no one was around to play with him.

One morning when the other children were at school, Tom's mother peered out the window to see Tom standing alone in the front yard. He was calling instructions to his two imaginary friends, George and Charlie, telling them where to stand. Betty Seaver watched as Tom ran toward a tree, turned and raced toward a spot some distance away. As he got closer, he slid, like a big league ballplayer. Then he jumped up, shrieking, "I'm safe! I'm safe!" just as if he was arguing with an umpire. Even without any other players, Tom still made himself part of a ball game.

Betty often read aloud to Tom. Her favorite book was *The Little Engine That Could*, a story about a tiny train that pushes itself up a long hill, saying to itself, "I think I can, I think I can, I think I can," until it tops the hill on sheer willpower. Even as a youngster, Tom wanted to win very much. He never stopped believing that he could. Until he was 12, he was a Little League pitching hero.

After three successful years as a Little Leaguer, Tom's ballplaying skills suddenly seemed to fade. He hadn't stopped concentrating or working hard. He hadn't stopped practicing. He had simply stopped growing. When he was 13, Tom saw his friends shoot up around him as he stayed 5'6''. His friends could all throw harder and run faster than Tom and suddenly he felt he had been left behind.

His size remained a problem until some time after he graduated from high school. Determined to help his father pay for his college education, Tom took a laborer's job at his father's company, and the physical effort added muscle to his body. Six months later, he joined the Marine Corps Reserve. After six months with the Marines, Tom was over six feet tall and weighed almost 200 pounds. When he returned to pitching at Fresno City College, his fastball exploded over home plate. By 1967, he was ready for a turn in the major leagues.

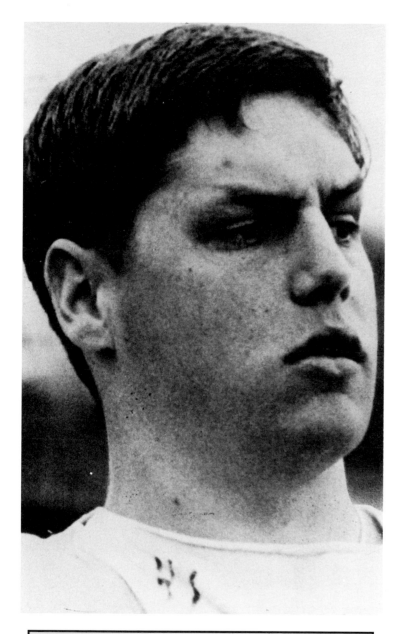

George Thomas Seaver was named Rookie of the year in 1967.

In July of 1969, almost 15 years to the day after he had pitched a perfect game as a Little Leaguer, Tom Seaver stood on the pitcher's mound at New York's Shea Stadium wearing the uniform of the New York Mets. The years of hard work had paid off. At the age of 24, Tom was the first real star of the Mets, who at the time were only in their eighth season in the National League. Thousands of fans crowded into the stadium to watch him pitch against the powerful Chicago Cubs, who were in first place in the National League East.

For the first few innings, Tom felt a stiffness in the shoulder of his pitching arm. He was throwing well, however, and setting the Cubs down in order. Despite their reputation for toughness at the plate, the Cubs couldn't get a hit off the man the Mets fans called "Tom Terrific."

As the innings rolled on, Tom continued to hold off the Cubs. Charles Seaver was in New York on business and was sitting in the stands, watching his son pitch. In the bottom of the eighth inning, when Tom stepped into the batter's box to hit, the stadium exploded in cheers and applause. Everyone knew that Tom Seaver was headed for a perfect game. All he needed was three more outs.

Tom could taste it. He had never wanted anything as much as he wanted this perfect game. Perfect games had only been thrown by 11 pitchers in the history of major league baseball. To be the 12th such pitcher would be an achievement to cherish forever.

Tom retired the first hitter in the top of the ninth. Next, young Jimmy Qualls stepped into the batter's box. He was a rookie and would not ordinarily have been in the lineup, but the Cubs regular centerfielder had made two costly errors the day before and manager Leo Durocher had yanked him from the lineup and put Qualls in his place.

Tom wound up for one of his trademark fastballs, known for the way they sank as they approached the plate. This pitch, however, did not sink. It came in hard and straight and Qualls swung and connected.

For just a moment, the ball hung in the summer air. Then it dropped on the grass in left centerfield. It was a clean single, the first hit of the game.

Tom's eyes misted. He turned his back to the plate for a moment, trying to collect himself. He had come *so* close to a perfect game in the major leagues! Would he ever come that close again? Years later he pitched a no-hitter, but never a perfect game.

In April of 1970 he pitched a remarkable game against the San Diego Padres, striking out 19 batters, including the final 10 in a row. This tied Steve Carlton's major league record of 19 strikeouts (set in 1969 against the Mets) and set a major league record for consecutive strikeouts. For some pitchers, it might have been a consolation for missing the chance of a perfect game, but not for Tom.

Afterward, talking about the game, Tom said, "It's fun to pitch a game like this . . . But [it] doesn't exhilarate me as much as a perfect game would have. That's the one I wish I had."

Tom pitched for the New York Mets until 1977, when he was traded to the Cincinnati Reds. Later, he returned briefly to the Mets before moving on to the Chicago White Sox and the Boston Red Sox. All told, he won 311 major league games.

In 1989, Tom became the first Mets player to have his uniform number, 41, retired by the club. No other Met will ever wear it again. Tom Seaver wasn't perfect, but he was frequently close.

TOM SEAVER'S CAREER HIGHLIGHTS:

- Rookie of the Year, 1967.
- National League Cy Young Award, 1969, 1973 and 1975.
- No-hit game, June 16, 1978 versus the St. Louis Cardinals.
- Made 12 All-Star Game appearances.
- NL Strikeout leader, 1970, 1971, 1973, 1975 and 1976.
- NL ERA leader, 1970, 1971 and 1973.

Ted Williams.

Darryl Strawberry.

CALIFORNIA DREAMIN'

Did you know that many of baseball's superstars were born or raised in California? In addition to growing beautiful fruit and vegetables, it seems California also grows talented ballplayers. Because the weather is warm so many months of the year, young players can spend more time on the ballfield and improve their chance of becoming major league players. Consider these Californians:

Walter Johnson (Fullerton)
Ted Williams (San Diego)
Jackie Robinson (Pasadena)
Joe DiMaggio (San Francisco)
Don Drysdale (Van Nuys)
Tom Seaver (Fresno)
Frank Robinson (Oakland)
Gary Carter (Culver City)
Keith Hernandez (San Francisco)
Kevin Mitchell (San Diego)
Eric Davis (Los Angeles)
Darryl Strawberry (Los Angeles)
Tim Leary (Santa Monica)
Steve Sax (Sacramento)
Barry Bonds (Riverside)

There are more current professional baseball players from California than any other state in the Union. How many more can you name?

During the 1980s, baseball continued to change. Even the field has changed. When Toronto moved into the Skydome in 1989, the Blue Jays became the 10th major league team to play their home games on an artificial surface. Half of the National League clubs play on artificial turf at home. Both players and balls move more quickly on artificial turf, which can make speed more important than power.

Pitching has also changed. The split-fingered fastball has become the weapon of choice for many hurlers, including Mike Scott of the Astros and Dave Stewart of the Athletics. In the '80s, the importance of relief pitchers continued to grow. Relief pitchers were no longer pitchers who weren't good enough to break into the starting rotation. Teams continued to redefine the jobs of men in the pen. Some teams had both righthanded and lefthanded middle relievers, righthanded and lefthanded setup men. Closers, also known as stoppers, aces and firemen, became some of the game's biggest stars. In the 1980s, these heroes included Dan Quisenberry, Bruce Sutter and Goose Gossage. In the '90s, bullpen aces include Dennis Eckersley of the Athletics and Dave Righetti of the Yankees.

Meanwhile, veteran Nolan Ryan of the California Angels keeps pitching—1990 marked his 24th major league season! At the beginning of the '80s, Los Angeles Dodgers pitcher Fernando Valenzuela became the first rookie to win the Cy Young award, and at the decade's close, Jim Abbott triumphed over a handicap to take to the pitching mound for the California Angels. In 1987 an amazing athlete, outfielder Bo Jackson became a superstar for both the Kansas City Royals and football's Los Angeles Raiders. In 1992, baseball will be an Olympic medal sport for the first time. Though baseball keeps changing, fans have retained their love of the game. As baseball heads into the 1990s, it is not only the all-American game, it's an international love affair.

Nolan Ryan has thrown six no-hitters, a major league record.

JOE AND THE NO-HITTER

Alvin, Texas, was brutally hot in the summer of 1958. The sun beat down relentlessly. The air was so humid it felt damp and mosquitoes buzzed around the fields.

None of that bothered the Little League players getting ready for their regular weekly game. The 11- and 12-year-old boys were much more interested in their warmups than in the warm weather. As long as they had a game to play, they didn't care how hot it was.

The two teams facing each other, the Lions and the Rangers, were both from Alvin. This game was particularly interesting because the opposing pitchers were close friends. The Lions pitcher was Joe Godwin. His friend, Nolan Ryan, was on the mound for the Rangers.

The two friends squared off against each other, each determined to win. Though they played together all the time, Joe and Nolan were both competitive pitchers. When it came to a Little League game, all they thought about was winning.

As the innings passed, Joe and Nolan both looked strong. Despite the brutal heat, no runs were scored by either side. Nolan began to worry as the game stretched toward the final innings. The Rangers hadn't scored a single run. Though he was shutting out the Lions, how was he going to win if his team didn't put any runs on the board?

It wasn't until close to the end of the game that Nolan began to realize what was happening. He had pitched another scoreless inning for the Rangers and sat down on the bench in the dugout. His teammates were excited, all of them talking at once. For a moment, Nolan didn't realize what they were saying.

"You're pitching a no-hitter!" his friends shouted at him. "The Lions haven't had a single hit since the game started!"

Nolan was happy about the idea that he might actually pitch a no-hit ball game. He pointed out to his teammates that it wouldn't do much good if he lost the game. After all, they didn't have a single run yet.

"Don't you get it?" his teammates shouted back at him. "You're not the only one pitching a no-hitter out there. Joe's pitching one, too!"

Wow! Nolan looked out at the mound, where Joe was firing strike after strike at the Rangers batters. Nolan hadn't realized how much Joe was fooling the Rangers. They were completely befuddled. When they did manage to hit something, it seemed to fly right into the glove of one of the Lions fielders.

Nolan knew he couldn't do much about Joe's game. He could only help his teammates by doing his best. It would be great to have a no-hitter, of course. But winning the game was more important, and he had to concentrate on that first.

As the final inning began, Nolan walked slowly out to the mound to face the Lions. He still felt strong, but he knew that if his team didn't score in the bottom of the inning, he would not win the game. Little League rules said that the game ended after six innings. There were no extra-inning games. The two good friends might just end up with a double no-hitter and a tie ballgame!

Nolan didn't want a tie. He wanted to win. He threw his best fastball past the three batters. In a few minutes, the Lions were retired and Nolan had his no-hitter!

Now the Rangers had their last chance against Joe Godwin. They dug in, hoping to get Nolan the win he wanted so much. Joe was tiring. He was so excited at the idea of throwing a no-hitter that his control was slipping.

Joe walked two Rangers. The next batter hit a drive into the outfield. The fielder made an error. Suddenly, the Rangers had the bases loaded!

Joe tried to pitch more carefully to the next batter. Like Nolan, he was thrilled by the idea of a no-hitter. He didn't want to throw anything that the batter could crack for a single.

With a count of three balls, Joe tried to slip a pitch past the hitter. The umpire signaled ball four. The Rangers hitter trotted to first base and the runner on third came home. The final score was 1–0. Joe had thrown a no-hitter, all right. He had also walked in the winning run!

Nolan was thrilled about winning the game, even though it meant beating one of his closest friends. It was his first no-hitter, though it wouldn't be his last.

Nolan was born in Texas in 1947. Between playing baseball and helping with the chores on his family's ranch, the young Texan grew tall and lean. His long arms developed amazing power and speed.

Nolan never seriously thought about pitching in the major leagues—that is, he didn't think about it until he pitched the no-hitter against the Alvin Lions. Like other boys, he'd dreamed of big league glory, but he didn't really think he had what it took to be a pro.

After the no-hitter in Little League, though, Nolan realized that he threw a very fast fastball, one that seemed to streak by the batters at the plate. In high school, he played on the varsity team where he pitched another no-hitter. He started to wonder whether he just might have the talent to play in the major leagues.

Soon after high school, Nolan was taken into the New York Mets farm system. By 1968, he was a member of the major league club in New York.

From the start, Nolan's major league career was exciting. Though he could not really throw a big league curveball, Nolan threw a fastball that was so extraordinary that he racked up impressive strikeout totals from his very first season.

Lynn Nolan Ryan pitched his first no-hitter in Little League.

At 22, in his third year in the major leagues, Nolan worked as both a starting pitcher and as a relief man, helping the Mets to their 1969 "miracle" finish, when they won the World Series in five games.

Yet Nolan knew he could be a better pitcher. He often had a sore arm because the Mets did not use him regularly. He also had a control problem. He threw hard, but he also threw all over the place. He knew he had to develop a curveball that would help him win consistently.

After the 1971 season, he was traded by the Mets to the California Angels. The Angels gave Nolan a chance to pitch every four days and Angels pitching coach Tom Morgan taught him how to throw a curveball. Nolan's curve only made his fastball look faster. Suddenly, Nolan Ryan was overpowering!

Through the years, pitching for several different ball clubs, he has remained overpowering. He has thrown a record six no-hitters, the most recent in 1990 against the Oakland A's. At 43, Nolan was the oldest pitcher to throw a no-hitter. He has struck out 19 batters in a game on three occasions and he also set a modern major league record for strikeouts in a season with 383 in 1973.

Even more impressive for such a hard-throwing pitcher is the fact that by the end of the 1990 season, Nolan had played in the major leagues for 24 seasons. In the mid-1970s, Nolan's fastball was clocked at 100.9 miles per hour, the fastest pitch on record.

Nolan takes his accomplishments in stride. His concern always is simply to get ready for his next start. As a Texas Ranger, he just keeps pitching no matter what the weather.

NOLAN RYAN'S CAREER HIGHLIGHTS:

- **Lifetime strikeouts—More than 5,000, a major league record.**
- **Six no-hitters, a major league record.**
- **American League strikeout leader, 1972–74, 1976–79 and 1989.**
- **National League strikeout leader, 1987 and 1988.**

SOUTH OF THE
BORDER SENSATION

The west coast of Mexico is flat desert country. Cactus grows freely and farming is difficult because the soil is poor. Whole families work long hours in the fields to earn enough money to subsist. When the local people aren't working, though, they love to watch baseball games. The local teams are very popular. People come to games to cheer for their teams and visit with their friends. It's always a happy afternoon at the ball field.

On one particular summer day in 1974, the people of Etchohuaquila were watching a new pitcher. He was the youngest son of the Valenzuela family. Four of his brothers—Francisco, Daniel, Gerardo and Manuel—were behind him on the field. If the young pitcher had trouble on the mound, his brothers were ready to help him out with a great play in the field.

Though he usually played first base, today young Fernando stood on the pitcher's mound. His brother Rafael was the team pitcher and another brother, Avelino, relieved Rafael when he got tired. Because he was usually so quiet and shy, Fernando's bold insistence that he be allowed to pitch had surprised his coach. But here he was at center stage in the middle of the diamond.

Fernando took a deep breath and looked at the first batter. He wasn't really sure he was ready for this challenge. But he was plenty old enough to pitch now. After all, he was 13, wasn't he? He was practically a man!

Fernando wound up, kicked his leg high—just like his brothers did—and delivered his first pitch. In a few minutes, the Etchohuaquila fans were peering at him in surprise. The kid was doing fine! Fernando pitched two innings and struck out two batters.

Fernando was excited and more than ready to go into the third inning, but the coach stopped him. He didn't like seeing young boys pitch too many innings. He

Fernando Valenzuela led the Dodgers to a World Series victory in 1981.

worried that they would ruin their arms. Fernando left the pitcher's spot after two innings, thrilled about his first pitching performance.

There were already 11 children in the Valenzuela household when Fernando Anguamea was born on November 1, 1960. His parents, Avelino and Maria Hermengilda, lived in a whitewashed adobe house with Fernando's six brothers and five sisters. The roof was thatched with mud and there was no electricity. The boys slept in the living room on a big mattress that doubled as a couch in the daytime. Fernando's parents and sisters shared the only bedroom. Fernando sometimes slept outdoors on warm summer nights. It was more comfortable than sharing a mattress with six brothers!

Etchohuaquila is a farming community where wealthy ranchers own most of the land. They often hire poorer people to farm the land for them. The older Valenzuela boys earned extra money as farmhands for the wealthy ranchers of Etchohuaquila. Fernando worked with his father and sisters in the family garden, growing beans and corn. Fernando hated the idea that one day he would have to join his brothers in the fields. He preferred to spend time by himself. When there was a lull in his chores, Fernando would often wander off alone and daydream.

When he wasn't helping out at home or going to school, Fernando played sports with his friends. Mexican boys learn two sports when they're very young: baseball and soccer. Fernando liked soccer, but it was not nearly as important to him as baseball was. Baseball felt natural to him. When one of his friends once asked him about baseball he answered, "God put the talent in my arm, not my feet."

By the age of 10, Fernando was scouring the corners of local baseball fields to find any balls that had been left behind. He insisted that the balls he found actually belonged to him. His friends, laughing, called him "Zurdo Robales," the lefthanded robber.

In the early 1970s, Etchohuaquila still did not have electricity in its homes. Then progress seemed to catch up with the town. Everyone was getting electric lights. Some were even getting television antennas! After being a hundred years behind the times for so long, the little community was catching up.

For the first time, the Valenzuela family was able to gather in the living room in the evenings to hear games of the Mexican Pacific Coast League broadcast on the radio. Mexican professional teams play all over the country and are as popular in Mexico as American teams are in the United States. Thousands of people come out to the stadiums to cheer for their favorite players. The Valenzuelas cheered from their own living room.

Listening to the games spurred Fernando to more daydreaming. These faraway players had once been poor boys like he was. If they could play professional baseball, why couldn't he? As he grew taller and stronger, Fernando put more and more effort into learning how to pitch. He loved pitching, and there was nothing he would rather do.

By May of 1976, when he was 15, Fernando was pitching regularly for the Etchohuaquila team. Etchohuaquila had won enough games to qualify for a regional tournament played 20 miles to the north in a town called Navojoa.

All the players on the team were excited. Fernando would be pitching the game.

They had seen Fernando strike out 16 players in one game and they felt confident of victory.

There were a number of important Mexican baseball men watching the tournament that day. One of them, Avelino Lucero, was responsible for choosing a team of all-stars from the state of Sonora. Since Etchohuaquila is in Sonora, Fernando was eligible to be chosen.

Lucero watched Fernando carefully during the game. Fernando impressed him, and Lucero chose him for his all-star team.

The Sonora all-stars played all-star teams from other Mexican states. In the second game of the all-star tournament, Sonora was in trouble. The score was tied, and the Sonoran pitcher had loaded the bases with no one out.

Lucero sent Fernando in to try to mop up the mess. Fernando had no lefthander's glove of his own. Usually he could borrow someone else's but this time he couldn't find one. So he grabbed a righthander's glove instead.

Though the crowd jeered the lefthanded pitcher who was using a righthander's glove, Fernando paid no attention. He bore down on the three batters that faced him. He retired all three. The other side didn't get a single run.

After a second all-star tournament in which Fernando was named Most Valuable Player, he was offered a contract for $250 to play for three months in the Mexican League. It was the chance of a lifetime and Fernando grabbed it. Though he had never lived away from home before, he wanted to play baseball more than anything. At the age of 15, Fernando became a professional ballplayer.

Life in the Mexican League was neither comfortable nor easy. Fernando often slept on the floor of the buses hired to take the players from one stadium to another. The stadiums were not as well-equipped as American fields are. The Tampico stadium, in fact, has railroad tracks running through the outfield. If a train comes through, the players have to stop the game!

Life was often lonely for the young pitcher from Etchohuaquila. He missed his family and friends back home. He was so shy that he had trouble making friends with his teammates, most of whom were older. Fernando spoke so little that the players were convinced he used sign language. He usually just nodded or shook his head to communicate.

But there were also things Fernando liked about his new life. Because he could now afford to eat better, he began to eat a lot. He also enjoyed the rich Mexican beer and drank plenty of it. As a result, the trim and muscular boy who had left Etchohuaquila was rapidly growing into a chubby young man. Fortunately, it didn't seem to affect his pitching. That powerful left arm snapped forward just as hard and fast no matter how much Fernando ate on the road.

In March of 1978, when Fernando was 17, his team played in Silao during Holy Week, the week between Palm Sunday and Easter Sunday. Since Mexico has many Catholic citizens, the ballparks were not as full as usual.

One man who did come to the ballpark was amazed at what he saw. Mike Brito, scout for the Los Angeles Dodgers, had come to watch the shortstop on the other team. Brito didn't think that much of the shortstop, but he liked Fernando.

Brito wanted to buy Fernando's contract right away. The team's owner told him that Fernando was too young to play major league baseball in the United States.

Fernando became a professional ballplayer while still in his teens.

He told Brito to check back in a couple of years.

The very next year, Al Campanis of the Dodgers flew down to Yucatan, where Fernando was now pitching. He offered once more to buy Fernando's contract. Mike Brito spent time with Fernando's family in Etchohuaquila, assuring the Valenzuelas that he would personally watch out for Fernando in the United States. The young pitcher would not be left alone in a country where he didn't even speak the language!

Finally, everyone agreed, and Fernando left Yucatan in July of 1979 for Lodi, California, where he would play on a Dodgers farm club. The following spring he reported to another Dodgers farm team in San Antonio, Texas. Late that season, he was called up by the Dodgers. He appeared in 10 games and didn't allow an earned run.

By 1981, he was really ready for the big leagues. A Dodgers pitching coach named Bobby Castillo had taught Fernando a screwball, which became the most important trick of his trade. Fernando was armed to face major league hitters.

The Dodgers that spring looked like a club that had just been through a natural disaster. By Opening Day, four of the regular pitchers were not ready to start a game. Fernando drew the Opening Day assignment because there was no one else to put in the rotation!

Fernando was as relaxed as he always was before a ball game. When the Dodgers finished batting practice, Fernando lay down on the training table and took a nap. By the end of the afternoon, he had given up only five hits to beat the Houston Astros, 5–0. He also had his first complete-game victory. The fans adored him. It was the beginning of "Fernando mania."

By the end of his rookie season, 20-year-old Fernando Valenzuela had captured the hearts of Dodgers fans. He had won 13 and lost 7, with a league-leading 180 strikeouts and eight shutouts!

Fernando capped his amazing first season by leading the Dodgers to a World Series victory. He was now so famous in Mexico that he had to sneak into his own wedding to avoid the mobs of fans waiting for him!

Fernando was the first rookie to win the Cy Young Award, an award for pitching excellence. He was also chosen Rookie of the Year in the National League. For Dodgers fans everywhere, Fernando was a great Mexican import.

FERNANDO VALENZUELA'S CAREER HIGHLIGHTS:

- Rookie of the Year, 1981.
- Cy Young Award, 1981 (1st rookie to win).
- Sporting News Player of the Year, 1981.
- Won Silver Bat (batting honor) for pitchers, 1981 and 1983.
- Did not allow a single earned run for the first 41⅓ innings of the 1985 season, a major league record.

All-around-athlete Bo Jackson prepares to take a swing for the Kansas City Royals.

A BOY FOR ALL SPORTS

The field was crowded with boys on that spring morning in 1972. It was the first day of the Little League season in McCullum, Alabama. Every boy there hoped to end up as the star of his team.

One of them, nine-year-old Bo Jackson, listened as the other boys talked about which positions they wanted to play. Most of the boys wanted to pitch. A few others wanted to play shortstop. Those were considered the flashiest and most glamorous positions, the ones that drew the most attention.

The coach looked over the boys crowding around him and asked for volunteers for each position. As he called out each position, boys yelled, "I'll do it!" "I want to!" "Me, me!" Most of the positions filled up quickly.

When the coach asked for a catcher, nobody volunteered. The coach waited for a moment. "Anybody want to be the catcher?" he asked again. There was still no answer.

Finally, Bo spoke up. "I'll do it." He had been eyeing the catcher's equipment: a chest protector, face mask, and shin guards. The catcher even wore his cap differently from the rest of the team, with the bill twisted around to the back of his head. Bo figured that out on the field with the other players, the catcher was easily the most noticeable person.

He liked the position for another reason as well. At the plate, the catcher was right in the middle of the action. Runners from third base had to get past him to score a run. He helped pitchers decide how to throw to batters. He was even the person who had to throw out a runner trying to steal second base!

Bo, wearing all that neat equipment, settled in happily behind the plate. The coach soon realized he had a problem.

Though he was the same age as the other boys, Bo was simply far too advanced for the rest of the team. Bigger than most of the others, he had a strong, accurate arm and surprising batting power at the plate. He could run faster, throw harder and bat better than anyone on the team. He could cut down almost any runner trying to steal and, when a runner tried to score from third base, Bo would block the plate with his whole body.

Two weeks into the season, the coach knew what he had to do. Though Bo loved playing in Little League, the coach took him aside and told Bo he would have to give up his spot on the team. "You're too rough to play with the others," the coach explained. "The others haven't grown as quickly as you have. You'll end up hurting somebody if you keep playing in Little League."

Bo was disappointed, but his coach promised that Bo wouldn't have to stop playing organized baseball. Bo was soon playing in Pony League, with boys 13 to 15 years old. Though Bo was six years younger than some of them, he had no trouble competing with the Pony League players.

Bo was one of ten children. He was born in Bessemer, Alabama, on November 30, 1962. His family was poor and struggled to earn enough money for rent and food.

Bo had no toys to play with so he made up his own games, picking up rocks in the streets and throwing them against walls and telephone poles. Day after day, he threw rocks. When he could throw them accurately from a short distance, he moved farther back. The more he practiced, the farther he could accurately throw the rocks.

Bo, however, had some personal troubles. Children in his neighborhood teased him because his parents weren't married and because he stuttered. Bo couldn't stand hearing his family called ugly names. He stuttered when he tried to respond to the insults, and then his tormentors teased him even more. Since Bo was big for his age, he decided to fight back. When kids teased him, he lashed out at them with his fists.

It was hard for Bo to express himself, especially since talking was such an effort for him. More and more, he simply fought his problems by punching and kicking. When he went to school, he was afraid to speak up in class. Even when he knew the right answer to a question, he stuttered so badly that he exhausted himself trying to speak.

It seemed as though Bo might be headed for a life of problems when he discovered organized sports. Bo was in third grade and he loved having teams with names and sometimes real uniforms with numbers on them. Everyone was the same age and played pretty much at the same level. As a third-grader Bo made the track team by outrunning fourth, fifth and sixth graders.

Bo began to realize that the energy he had used to fight could become power on a playing field. He felt good about himself when he threw a ball high in the air or ran a race as fast as he could. The other boys stopped tormenting him and began admiring him for his athletic accomplishments.

When Bo saw this, his life began to change. His stuttering became less of a problem, and disappeared in a few years. He was finding out that he had a special gift.

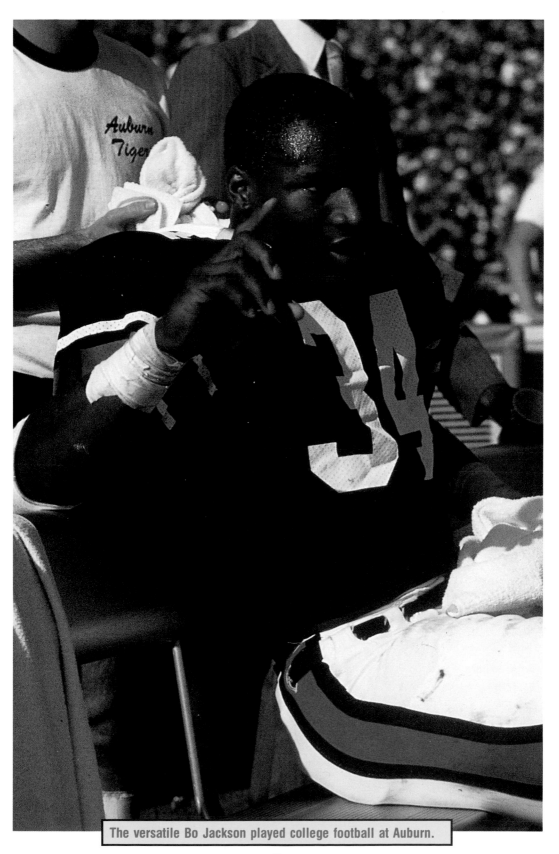

The versatile Bo Jackson played college football at Auburn.

The gift was sometimes too much of a good thing. Because of his rapid growth and excellent coordination, Bo was way ahead of the boys his own age and many who were a lot older.

After Bo had played in Pony League for about a month, one of his older brothers had an idea. The industrial team in town was made up of 18- to 20-year-old players who were all hoping to be spotted by a professional baseball scout. The team needed a catcher and Bo's brother figured that the 9-year-old Bo was good enough to catch for his team, even if he was a lot smaller than the other team members. Bo agreed to play.

In Pony League Bo had developed a trick that astonished everyone. Bo could actually throw a ball from home plate to second base without standing up. The ball left his hand while he was still crouched on his knees!

For a while, no one realized just how good Bo was because he seemed so young. Fans would yell at the coaches, telling them to get "that baby" off the field before he got hurt!

Bo never let on to opposing batters that he could play his position so well. When batters reached first base, they looked at the little boy behind the plate and figured they could steal second easily. Bo always let them take second.

Before long, the runners would decide to try for third. As soon as they left for third, Bo would whip back his arm and gun the ball to the third baseman, without ever rising from his knees. The runners never had a chance. When they walked back to the dugout after Bo's throw, they were shaking their heads. It was hard to believe a boy could throw so hard without even standing up!

By the time he was 12, Bo was playing regularly with the men's teams around town. As he grew older, he also joined teams at high school, where baseball was only one of several sports offered. By the time he graduated from high school, Bo was also playing football and track and field!

This interest in variety stayed with Bo at Auburn University, where he not only excelled at baseball, but where he won the Heisman Trophy in 1985 as the country's outstanding college football player. Baseball was still Bo's first love, and he joined the Kansas City Royals in 1986.

The challenge still wasn't enough. Though only a few athletes have ever attempted to play more than one sport professionally at the same time, Bo signed a football contract in 1987 to play with the Los Angeles Raiders. In the summer he was an outfielder and in the fall he was a running back.

During baseball's 1989 All-Star Game, the Nike shoe company broadcast a new commercial. It showed various athletic stars paying tribute to Bo Jackson as a man who knew many sports. "Bo knows baseball . . . Bo knows football . . . Bo knows basketball . . ." It was a funny commercial, based on the image of a superstar who seemed to be able to do everything.

That night, Bo played on the American League All-Star team at Anaheim Stadium in Anaheim, California. In the first inning, he slammed a 433-foot home run. It was an important hit in the game, and Bo was named the All-Star Game's Most Valuable Player.

Today, Bo and his wife are working to help children who grew up in the same tough circumstances in which he did. Sports gave him a chance to make something good of his life. He wants to be sure others get a chance, too.

It's true that Bo knows baseball and Bo knows football. Most importantly, though, Bo knows who he is and what he wants.

BO JACKSON'S CAREER HIGHLIGHTS:

- **All-Star Game Most Valuable Player, 1989.**
- **32 home runs and 105 RBIs, 1989.**

Jim Abbott's pitching was so brilliant that he went straight from college to the major leagues.

AN OLYMPIAN FEAT

By the time Jim Abbott was seven years old, he knew that he loved sports. Along with the other boys in his neighborhood in Flint, Michigan, he spent his time after school playing baseball and football.

Kathy and Mike Abbott were not surprised when Jim came home one day and announced that he wanted his own baseball glove. Jim was their only child and they wanted to give him every advantage they could. Jim's father held jobs as both a meat packer and a car salesman. Money wasn't a problem. The Abbotts knew that almost every boy Jim's age wanted a baseball glove. But Jim was not exactly your average boy. Jim had been born with a right arm that ended at the wrist. He had no right hand.

James Anthony Abbott was born on September 19, 1967. He was a sunny-faced, happy child, but Mike and Kathy couldn't help worrying about him. Jim couldn't hold anything with his right arm. He used his left hand to eat and hold a pencil.

When he was five, Jim was fitted with an artificial hand. His parents thought it would make his life easier, but Jim was uncomfortable and felt awkward using the hand. He hated it.

After a year and a half, Jim told his parents he didn't want to use the hand. Other parents might have insisted that Jim keep it, but Mike and Kathy told him it was all right to take it off. Jim preferred to work with the arms he had been born with.

It wasn't always easy for Jim. Children in the neighborhood sometimes teased him about his right arm, and Jim would come home crying. His parents would listen to him, dry his tears and send him out to play again. They taught him to be brave about his handicap.

By the time Jim was old enough to ask for a baseball glove, he already knew how to throw a baseball lefthanded. When Kathy wondered if Jim might not be able to keep up with other kids, he insisted he could. His parents gave in and bought him his first glove.

Jim set up a pitching area behind his house. He began to pitch against a high wall in the yard. Jim's favorite pitcher was Nolan Ryan, who always struck out a lot of batters with his blazing fastball. As Jim threw against the wall, he pretended he was Ryan, striking out lineup after lineup.

Jim also practiced a technique for using his new glove. A lefthanded pitcher always wears his glove on the right hand. Since Jim had no right hand, he learned to hold his glove on the end of his right arm as he pitched the ball, and then to quickly slip his glove onto his left hand to catch the ball when it came back at him. Over the years, he practiced this move so often that it became second nature.

Jim never considered himself handicapped. To him all the relentless practice was simply what an athlete had to do. A great competitor had to practice and hone his skills. He had to try to identify his weaknesses and learn to minimize them.

Although he was still a boy, Jim judged himself by the standards of a professional. What were his weak spots? Where were the problems that might give the batter an advantage over him? How could he overcome his flaws?

When Jim was in high school, he was a star athlete. Not only did he pitch for the varsity baseball team, he also became the football team's starting quarterback.

As a pitcher, he threw four no-hitters in four years. As a quarterback, he led his teammates to the state semifinals. In one game he threw four touchdown passes!

By the time Jim was a high school senior, both college and professional scouts were asking him to play for their teams. The Toronto Blue Jays asked him to sign a professional baseball contract with them and the University of Michigan offered him a scholarship to play in Ann Arbor.

Jim chose Michigan. His baseball coach thought Jim was such an excellent player that he sometimes put him into the game as a designated hitter. This was a tremendous compliment for two reasons. First, most pitchers don't spend much time working on their hitting skills and are less likely to be good batters than players who bat every day. Second, Jim could only grip the bat with his left hand. During one game as a designated hitter, Jim had two hits in four at bats!

Jim won the 1987 Sullivan Award as the best amateur athlete in the United States and his performance at the University of Michigan brought him the opportunity to pitch for the U.S. baseball team in the 1987 Pan American Games. Jim turned in an outstanding performance at the Pan Am Games, winning two games for the U.S. without surrendering a single earned run! He also carried the American flag during the opening ceremonies.

Jim's play in 1987 helped earn him a spot in the 1988 Summer Olympic Games in Seoul, Korea. Though the Olympic officials did not award official medals for the baseball competition, the teams played fiercely. The Americans felt particularly driven to do well, since baseball is considered a particularly American pastime.

In the final game of the Olympic tournament, the United States played Japan for the championship. Jim took the mound as the starting pitcher. Though international reporters focused on the story of his missing right hand, Jim concentrated on the Japanese batters and won the game for the United States.

After the Olympics, Jim returned to Michigan and waited for the annual draft of college baseball players. Though he won the Golden Spikes Award as the best player in amateur baseball, he began to hear odd complaints about his performance.

Jim Abbott was a star pitcher in college despite the disadvantage of having only one hand.

Some of the professional scouts told him plainly that they wondered about his ability to hit and field. Would having only one hand keep him from playing his position effectively? No matter how good his pitching was, major league teams might not take a chance on him if they thought he was a weak fielder.

Jim felt nervous now. It was the first time since childhood that he had given much thought to being a player with only one hand. He knew he could pick off a runner who strayed too far from a base. He knew he could field bunts and throw batters out. He could even bunt himself, when necessary. What if the pro teams didn't see the situation his way?

Apparently, the pros weren't all that worried about Jim. The California Angels drafted him as eighth pick in the first round of the draft, and Jim became a hot news item all over again. At the Angels' spring training camp in 1989 he was a great human interest story for reporters. His pitching was so brilliant in spring training that the Angels decided not to send Jim down to the minors. Straight out of college, Jim Abbott was headed for the major leagues!

Jim was a little nervous about starting his career at the top. Fortunately, he didn't seem to need much time to adjust. He just got down to business winning ball games for the Angels. Jim was on his way to becoming a major league star.

Jim Abbott is a highly competitive athlete who always demands the best from himself. He's not interested in being a public figure. He wants only to be the best pitcher he can be.

His sense of humor is a great asset. His attitude remains the same as it was when local reporters interviewed him as a high school senior. One of them asked Jim how he got to be such an amazing high school athlete.

Jim grinned at him. "Whenever I get too impressed with myself," he answered, "I try to remember that I didn't get here singlehandedly." Then he burst out laughing, before adding, "I've been saving that line since seventh grade!"

JIM ABBOTT'S CAREER HIGHLIGHTS:

- **1988 Olympics, winning U.S. pitcher in the final game verses Japan.**
- **1987 Pan Am Games, won two games with an ERA of 0.00.**
- **Sullivan Award as outstanding amateur athlete in the United States, 1987.**
- **Golden Spikes Award as best amateur baseball player, 1987.**
- **Ended rookie season as a California Angel with a 12–12 record, 1989.**